Adeyemo Temidayo

The *Family* GOD'S Work of Restoration

ISBN: 978-978-50012-3-5

Unless otherwise stated, all scripture quotations in this book are taken from the New King James Version of the Bible.

Printed in the Federal Republic of Nigeria by:
NiU Nation Publishers
The New Nation Centre
Block 6E, Zone D, OAU Central Market
Ile Ife - Nigeria
Email: niunationpublishers@gmail.com
Tel/whatsapp: 0803 854 8073

DEDICATION

To the seed, the first-fruit company, whom the Lord will use to trigger a holy movement that will bring back the Ark into Its rightful place: our homes.

PREFACE TO THE 2011 EDITION

Two important clarifications need be made from the word, go. First, this book does not focus primarily on marriage or family issues – contrary to what may be initially assumed. Rather, it seeks to enlighten the Christian public on God's restoration agenda, in the hope that very fundamental issues regarding Assembly (popularly called church) life and practice today may be revisited.

However, you will discover, as you read, it is impossible to speak about God's program of restoration without bringing the family under spotlight, since it plays an indispensable role in both the means and the end of the restoration process.

Second, the issues raised and positions expressed in this book are not exhaustively discussed. This is meant to be an appetizer to stimulate readers to explore the topic further. At the end of this book, there are other recommended readings that shed more light and bring the sincere seeker into higher levels of accuracy.

Please, feel free to send feedback to the author. These will facilitate collective learning and also provide more content for other works in the pipeline.

PREFACE TO THE NEW EDITION

In view of my current understanding and conviction of the meaning of *Ekklesia* and my knowledge of the sheer historical fact of the mistranslation of the word *Ekklesia* to Church, I have painstakingly gone through the entire script in order to change the word, *Church*, to *Assembly* (or simply leave it as *Ekklesia*) when referring to a body of believers. I however retain the word, *church*, to mean either the literal building or Christian religious organisations and denominations. See Inset 3 in Page 92 for further details.

ACKNOWLEDGMENTS

I shall ever be thankful to the Lord for using several teachers of His word to shape my understanding of the family and God's program of restoration: Brothers Bankole Akinmola, Kola Adegoke, Sam Tukura, Noel Woodroffe, Emeka Nwankpa, Mike Oye – just to mention a few. Thank you all for answering God's call to be a blessing to the nations.

To the Kingdom community in which I experienced, first hand, the reality of the communal life of the Ekklesia between 1999 and 2005. Members (immediate and extended) of this community are today scattered in various parts of the world. May this book revive your passion for that glorious vision of Zion's emergence which engulfed our hearts and we gave ourselves unreservedly to. May each one of us come into a progressive revelation of the Lord's eternal purpose and may we find our place in the fulfilment of that purpose, amen.

In 2015, I was privileged to visit the US to participate in an informal training on planting organic expressions of the Ekklesia facilitated by Milt Rodriguez. That period of training exposed me the more to the understanding of God's eternal purpose, as taught by forebears like Austin Sparks, Watchman Nee and Witness Lee. I also met Henry Hon who has become a wonderful friend and co-worker in the vision and practice of God's eternal purpose from house to house. Meeting you brothers has been a real blessing!

My co-labourers in the Lord's vision of planting, nurturing and strengthening organic Kingdom communities (code-named *Project Ekklesia*) in different parts of Nigeria and beyond: you have continued to fuel my inspiration. Especially to the saints in Ibadan; more often than not, you have had to play the dual role of being my co-workers and a local expression of the Ekklesia in your city. Together, we shall see the travail of our soul and we shall be satisfied.

Professor Alfred Adegoke - whom we call Brother Fred. Your shepherding heart is indeed outstanding. Thank you for being there always, and for writing an awesome Foreword.

To my family, where God has taught us many profound things, as we gather together at the feet of the Master every morning. We are a living proof of the fact that a devotion a day keeps the devil away.

To you who will read this book with an open heart and choose to wholly follow the Lord, no matter the cost.

God bless you all, amen.

Temidayo

TABLE OF CONTENTS

FOREWORD

In the Bible, the word "Church"[1] (actual Greek word: *Ekklesia*) means "the called out ones"; it means a company of people. For a long time, however, this word has been taken incorrectly to mean a building. It is very clear from the account in Acts that the first century believers met in homes. During the time of Jesus, common ordinary dwelling places were used for the building up of one another in love and even to spread the gospel.

Undue emphasis on elaborately and ornately designed churches appears to be the order of the day. In some cases, these buildings have themselves become objects of worship. Hundreds of millions of naira have been expended on building and maintaining these "sacred" buildings.

It is important to note that having buildings for worship was not a topic for discussion among the pioneer believers. They did not have any building during their period of greatest advance. In fact, churches did not appear until the year 232 AD. The most explosive period of church growth in history took place during the period of the pioneer Christian Assembly (early "church") when structure, bureaucracy and organization were virtually

---

[1] More clarification on "church" is given in Inset 3 (Page 91)

non-existent.

How then did the early Lord's Assembly maintain such high and enviable standard of Christian witness and testimony both within and without - which Christendom today with all our paraphernalia of ministry and sophisticatedness are still struggling to attain? The sincere believer who knows the scripture well will not fail to observe that back then, Ekklesia was closest to the family. In fact, the Assembly was family and every Christian family was an assembly.

This literary effort by Adeyemo Temidayo seeks to reawaken Believers today to that critical place that the family occupied in Assembly life and practice, with the hope that believers all over the world and particularly in our nation, Nigeria, would begin to respond to this trumpet call of God to return to the divine order; to move away from institutionalized, stereotyped and heavily politicized Christianity to the realm of worshipping God in spirit and in truth.

It is very instructive that it was when the early Assembly moved away from the living rooms and homes of the brethren to buildings and complex organizational structures that the momentum got lost. Christendom today is guilty of the same - and this book calls for a change. May the Spirit of God speak calmly and refreshingly into your heart as you read, and grant grace to you to follow the recommendations shared herein.

ADEGOKE, Alfred
Professor of Counselling Psychology
University of Ilorin, Nigeria

INTRODUCTION

Allow me to make a confession: I am not a marriage specialist. I do not even consider myself qualified to write a book on marriage. In my early years as a Christian, marriage issues never caught my fancy; I never took marriage seminars seriously. As a matter of fact, I used to look at those who were eager to attend such seminars as not-so-spiritual. My thinking was that marriage is something that would come as naturally as growing hair in one's armpit when the time comes; it should not require any fuss.

Of course, I was quite young then and therefore inexperienced. Today, with about 16 years in the field of play, I believe I now know much better than that position of naivety I held about 22 years ago. In fact, today, I naturally have a revered regard for anyone, Christian or otherwise, who has successfully kept the marriage vows for 20 years – and still counting – though a number of cases all around us have proved beyond every shadow of doubt that in marriage, just as it is with the salvation of the soul, no one can really claim to have arrived. It is *"he who endures to the very end"* that can be justified.

In fact, one need not be an extra-spiritual Christian to be concerned about the situation with marriages in recent times. It is alarming and justifiably worrisome! Early in 2011, I was devastated with the news of an elderly Christian couple well known to me who called off their marriage of over 25 years! The couple were both products of the evangelistic revival of the 60's and had some input in my Christian discipleship. I could never imagine that a marriage that long could end up on the rocks - let alone among Christians so mature.

I began to realize that those many years before the eventual split, their marriage would have been anything but pleasant.[1] But these would never have been noticeable by fellow church members, neighbours and colleagues at work. It gave me a reason to believe that many couples who come to church and smile so beautifully when interacting with other brethren and even attend couples fellowship together could be moaning under the pressure and yet doing their best to cover up because, after all, Christians aren't supposed to have marriage problems. The worst fear of the average "old school" believer is to have a soiled testimony marriage-wise (the new generation folks don't seem to care that much). So for years, they keep 'coping' till the bubble bursts.

But to compound the situation further, the elderly brother chose to remarry another divorcee whose Christian roots also dated back to the late 60's!

But this is only a child's play to what obtains in other climes. December 31, 2009, I got a shock of my life when I learnt that my own beloved Ray Boltz[2] had divorced his wife of 35years on the grounds that he could no longer fight his urge for same-sex

---

[1] To be fair on this couple, there was a major health challenge that brought a new twist to the case. Though not an excuse, I hold the view that but for this challenge, their marriage could have remained Heaven on earth.

[2] I first heard Ray Boltz' *Feel the Nails* in 1995 and was completely blown away by the depth of his lyrics coupled with his sheer creativity. Ever since, I have devoured anything from him: *A Concert of a Lifetime, No Greater Sacrifice, Honor and Glory* etc. Some of his hits include *I Pledge Allegiance to the Lamb, The Hammer* and *Thank you for Giving to the Lord.* Sadly today, his latest albums promote the LGBT agenda. Remember him in your prayers

affections. In fact, according to him, he had lived a lie almost his entire life and it was time to embrace who he really was. In other words, just like the husband of a dear woman of God, Christie Moore[3], he left his wife not for another woman but for another man!

The above instances, among so many, have made the concern for Christian marriages to grip my heart. I began to say to myself: keeping one's marriage is not at all to be assumed as something automatic; it is hard work! One cannot but conclude that the hordes of hell have been given marching orders to discredit Christian homes at all cost - particularly the homes of ministers! All these have made strong impressions upon my heart regarding the gravity of the subject of marriage particularly in this end time.

I cannot forget a stage play I watched some 30 years ago by Calvary Love Drama Group. I still remember the title, *"The Evil that Men Do"*, staged at the S.O.N Auditorium, UCH, Ibadan. At the beginning of the play, an 'old man' narrator quoted II Timothy 3:3 with the emphasis on 'truce breakers', stressing that this is one sin that would become very rampant in the end time. Probably, that was the first time I ever heard the word, truce. But I was able to gather from his explanation or from the body of the play that it meant covenant.

Though it has been over three decades, that play and the concept of truce have refused to leave my mind. Today, it is clear that the present generation does not understand what commitment means: whether to God, in marriage or relationships generally, at work, in churches and so on. In the West, the concept of 'partnering' is now the acceptable alternative to marriage.

Paradoxically, these grim realities the institution of marriage is

---

[3] Christie Moore herself said this when she came to Nigeria in 1993. But that was 26years ago. Who knows, the man may have repented.

faced with were not what drew my heart to the subject of the family – I would rather leave that to seasoned marriage counsellors. My burning bush experience started around March 2011 during a Sunday fellowship. As we chorused the song, *'Ancient of Days, forever the same'*, I noted with a little sense of sadness that a number of things about Christendom today have changed a great deal from what they used to be in the Assembly of the first century. One of such among many is the structure that defines our fellowshipping or gatherings.

About 12 years earlier, through a very unique Kingdom experience that I was opportune to be part of, the Lord showed us that the Body of Christ actually started from homes and as we journey closer towards the end, she will return to homes. This assertion is in line with what Watchman Nee, Gene Edwards, Wolfgang Simson and several other notable men have written on the subject.

Needless to say, Christianity has long left the living rooms into large exotic halls and the popular argument is that the pattern adopted by the pioneer Assembly of believers was necessitated by the prevailing conditions they were subject to at the time. So, convicted by the lyrics of the song, I, in my mind, flipped through the books of the Bible from Genesis to Revelation, in an attempt to find out if the concept of "Ekklesia in homes" was a happenstance of the early Christians or an actual representation of the divine blueprint.

Before this time, I had encountered various understandings which gave me a good idea that marriage/the family is a core course, as far as the University of Pleasing God is concerned; and that once you register for it, failure is not an option. Sometime between 1997 and 1999, this maxim crystallised upon my heart: the love of money is not as much the root of evil as a bad marriage. Earlier, in 1995, I had heard Engr. Kola Adegoke say in a message that those who violate the marriage covenant fail to understand that they are tampering with a divine working, marriage being an institution meant to reflect the relationship between Christ and His Ekklesia. Paul said, *"This is a great mystery, but I speak concerning Christ and the Assembly."* (Eph. 5:31)

Yet earlier that same year (February, actually), Dr. Noel Woodroffe was unequivocal: God first, family second, ministry third! Incidentally, I heard Pastor Bank Akinmola repeat exactly the same thing. Ever since, I have heard this paraphrased in different ways again and again. It was however from Pastor Bank that I first learnt that the divine imperative is to use the family structure to bring His blessings to the nations, drawing his analysis from God's covenant with Abraham in Genesis 12. I cannot forget what Dr. Mike Oye said in 2008, that the Christian home is the first Assembly and is recognised by God even more than our church organizations.

This was the background against which I ran through the scriptures in my mind even while we sang the song. As I went from one portion of scripture to the other, which I will share with you in this book, it became crystal clear to me that the family structure as God's vehicle for replenishing the earth is consistent throughout scripture and this fact alone makes it worthy of our collective attention.

That was in March. But a little earlier than that, soon after our Special Jubilee Congress in October 2010 and our Emerging Leaders Retreat – February 2011, I had begun to feel a gentle frustration over what I felt was a slow pace at getting our message across in spite of our continued tri-annual meetings. Of what use is it then – my heart seemed to cry out – for how long oh Lord, will we continue these meetings without seeing the eventual rise of a Kingdom generation?

In response, the Lord directed me to begin to focus on reaching out to specific families and discipling them in a Kingdom way. It was then that He showed me that until any revelation, truth or instruction of the Spirit is received and applied at the family level, such truth cannot become established and widespread. At that instant, faster than the speed of thought, several scriptural instances akin to my March experience began to flood my heart to validate this assertion. Again, I will share these with you in this book.

This insight, as it were, became a seal on the March meditation and I saw quite clearly that there was a direct connection between the family institution and God's program of restoration; that the family goes beyond a mere human institution for procreation and socialisation but is, according to Barrister Emeka Nwankpa, "God's template for discipling the nations". Intuitively, I knew it was time to set the trumpet to the mouth.

I took the pain and space to narrate all that just to bring us to this point: The Kingdom of God and Heaven's age-long agenda to see it restored here on earth as it is in heaven and in the pre-fallen world takes the centre-stage in this book.

Having said that, I seem to hear a mild protest in my mind: "Look, hurting families need healing; helping homes to get along and to avoid breakdown, coping with recalcitrant kids, financial pressure and other pressing marital challenges are stirring at us in the face – yet here you are talking about something else!"

I agree that the issues mentioned above – and much more besides – are very real and need to be addressed. Thankfully, as I alluded to earlier, there are a good number of ministries devoted to this and may more emerge. Be that as it may, I believe the subject of restoration is related to these challenges more or less.

How, you may ask? Well, the problems we seek answers to which many marriage counsellors and seminars try to address are only bi-products of a cloaked but more foundational problem. It is common knowledge that "Purpose unknown, abuse inevitable". We shall get to see in this book that these varying and often highly embarrassing challenges we face are as a result of our failure to understand the very purpose the Initiator of the family institution had in mind at creation.

Thus, my passionate prayer is that the Lord will use this book to redirect our focus as husbands, wives, fathers, mothers, children and kindred to the Kingdom of God as the primary essence of the family and seek with all our seeking to make our homes, in the words of Wolfgang Simson, "houses that changed the world."

A NEW DAY DAWNS

I see a new day dawn over the whole earth
Ekklesia arising in the light of His presence
His glory arising over the Lord's House
The stars of God ushering in a new season
A people filled with His life, walking in truth
Set to do the will of the King of all creation

Weary of man's way, seeking afresh Zion's way
Travelling the path, they pave the way for
A mighty host from every tongue and tribe
Yearning to see His face, the Desire of nations

And in Zion, I see the King appear
His people spread out before Him
Joy and laughter with praise & thanksgiving
Hand in hand, boys and girls run along the streets
The envy of the whole earth is Zion
A heavenly culture, the Kingdom civilisation
Even so let it be, even in our days - amen.

CHAPTER ONE

THE RESTORATION AGENDA: AN OVERVIEW

What is the Central Goal of Christianity?

Let me start by asking a question which exposes a serious concern: what is the central essence of scripture and Christianity? My concern stems from the fact that what I have discovered for myself, after several years of seeking, is a far cry from the popular theme which has been built over the decades into the Christian psyche. Put simply, Christianity as projected today revolves round accepting Jesus, making effort to live a holy life, serving God in a church and then waiting till one dies and goes to heaven or when God decides that the world should come to an end.

In-between this general theme (our being saved here on earth and our eventually going to heaven), we do quite a whole lot of things: we heal; we exorcise; we teach on prospering and motivate ourselves to achieve; we proselytise and plant churches; we develop various ministries; we build institutions - we do so many things. Furthermore, we polarise ourselves along several lines and claim that one is better over another; we fight one another and try to patent God so that anyone who needs Him would have to come to our own particular group.

We do so many things some of which appear to conflict themselves, that any absolutely neutral person who wants to make an objective choice (without necessarily reading the bible personally) would easily get confused! And in the midst of it all, we only seem to be going in circles. The lamentation of the preacher in Ecclesiastes 1 describes us so well:

> *"All the rivers run into the sea, yet the sea is not full... That which has been is what will be, that which is done is what will be done, and there is nothing new under the sun."* — Eccl. 1:7,9

With our numerous and diverse ministry activities, churching and all, the sea is not yet full. We look into society and ask ourselves, what has changed, really? All our lofty claims of exploits are hardly verifiable and it appears that our impact on those systems humanity revolves round is very minimal. Society today seems to be darker than ever before and is positioning itself to be more and more secular (without God). In short, we have a big problem with authenticity!

Above all, our ultimate goal, which has also become free for all, is still very far from our grasp – whether you wish to pitch your tent with perfection, Christ-like maturity, the glorious Assembly, immortality, or possessing the seven mountains, total dominion or world evangelization, personal holiness and so on. And this is despite the much touted claim that God does not need a crowd to do His work.

So I reason: if He doesn't, why then has your own group (or mine) not been able to produce that needed few to get the job done and trigger off the long-awaited revival? Invariably, it appears that none of us has it totally figured out after all; no one has the proverbial magic wand. Each of us seems to be only doing what we know to do best while we wait for when God Himself, as it were, would put an end to this sin-ridden world or whisk His people away.

This dismal but factual state of things within Christendom was what prompted me into trying to find a simple and straightforward answer to just one question that our several positions have not helped to answer: what is God really about? Some will say discipleship is it; some will say it is missions; some will say He is raising a glorious Assembly; some will say until every nuke and cranny of the earth is filled with churches. Yet others will say He is raising mature sons; and yet some others, God wants Christianity to dominate in every sphere of human endeavour. And though some of these dovetail into each other, we all have different ideas as to how to go about these things. So, what exactly does the bible say and not necessarily what I am inundated with from all fronts?

Well, in due course, through a combination of personal study and listening to/reading many others, it pleased the Lord to beam His light of understanding into my heart to the point that I arrived at a very definitive position on the subject; and I was also helped to articulate what was shown to me. Thus, I describe the divine agenda by firstly bringing it under two headlines: His ultimate purpose and His present purpose(s).

God's ultimate purpose is His overall intention for creation which was set forth in Himself before the world began. Consider the following scriptures:

> *"Having made known to us the mystery of His will, <u>according to His good pleasure which He purposed in Himself</u>. that in the dispensation of the fullness of the times He might gather together in one all things in Christ, both which are in heaven and which are on earth – in Him."* —Eph. 1:9-10

> *"To the intent that now the manifold wisdom of God might be made known by the church to the principalities and powers in*

the heavenly places, <u>according to the eternal purpose which He accomplished in Christ Jesus our Lord</u>." — Eph. 3:10-11

"But we speak the wisdom of God in a mystery, the hidden wisdom <u>which God ordained before the ages</u> for our glory." — 1 Cor. 2:7

His present purpose however has to do with everything God is doing which was occasioned by the fact of the fall of man. While the former is the ultimate end, the latter is a means to that end. Consider this example: a founder of a corporation puts up a free healthcare scheme for the benefit of his staff. This is so that if any of his workers fall ill, they can receive speedy treatment in order to resume work and not jeopardise production. Thus, all the provisions of the health scheme are not an end in themselves but a means to an end.

In the same way, concepts like reconciliation, atonement, redemption, salvation of the soul and preparing the bride are all part of His present purpose, which He is carrying out in time – because they are all means to arriving at His overall eternal purpose. However, most of Christendom have been engrossed with only certain aspects of His present purpose without realising that they are actually a means to an end. For instance, when the question is asked, "What is God really about?" the answer usually given to that is "Oh, to seek and save the lost."

However, what should immediately come to our mind is, "Could that have been the original intention behind creation? What if Adam never fell, and so, needed no saving?" This singular perspective should make us see that saving the lost is but a means; because God actually had a purpose which man was meant to serve before the fall happened. Not recognizing the overall eternal purpose of God beyond the present purposes more often than not has led us into mistaking the means for the end.

And this is why once we are able to get someone converted and committed to a church, what else is there? We believe that's it. Thereafter, all our efforts are channelled towards whatever will retain them in church – by creating activities that will keep them engaged and by serving them titillating messages all year round. Check the contents of most pastors' sermons 52 Sundays a year and our special conferences and conventions: they are mostly centred on how to get God to bless us more and ultimately make heaven.

Invariably, we abuse the means by focusing on them as the end. This was the case with the children of Israel when they turned into a golden calf the gold ornaments they came out of Egypt with. God had a purpose for asking them to plunder the Egyptians, which He would later reveal in Exodus 25:1-9. But not knowing the purpose, the very blessing became an object of idolatry. May we be instructed by this.

So, everything that we do in the sphere of time should be in the context of bringing us back to that original intention which He had purposed in Himself before the creation of the world.

Having stressed the need for a clear understanding of God's overall purpose, call it the eternal purpose, frequently used in the writings of Austin Sparks, Watchman Nee and Witness Lee; or the ultimate intention, as DeVom Fromke puts it in His book, *"The Ultimate Intention"*, that is not directly our focus in this book – though we will gloss over it as we attempt to define the term "Restoration".

Rather, in addressing the very first question we started out with - what exactly is God about - we want to focus more on the second headline which I called "His present purposes". I believe this is the focus of virtually everything recorded for us from the end of Genesis 3 to the beginning of Revelations 21 - which I wish to summarise with one singular word: **restoration**. The Bible, in essence can be titled, God's restoration agenda.

I am particularly endeared to that term out of the other words in my Christian consciousness: Revival, Reformation, Renewal, Awakening and so on. It stuck to me since I read Bryn Jones, *"The Radical Church"* during my service year in 2003. I like it because it already takes into account the fact that it is only a means to an end. The term, "Restoration" points to something outside itself. It invokes in the mind, the consciousness that something fell out of place but needs to be brought back to its original position. So, in a very good sense, the word restoration conveniently links the end to the means, thereby showing dimensions of the divine working to be one.

Consequently, I feel safe to say that the singular narrative of the entire bible is the story of restoration being played out. And if this is so, Christianity should be about one thing chiefly: restoration. Everything we do in Christendom ought to be centred on that theme else it is a waste of time in the long run.

Unfortunately, the popular theme, which we had described earlier, has little to do with restoration. Rather, it seems to give the impression that God, having realised that He cannot win the war over the earth, considered His best option is to take the few people who manage to believe in Him out of the earth into Heaven and then in utter frustration destroy the earth and those miserable unbelievers – so that His own people can live happily ever after in their heavenly mansions, taking a stroll down the streets of gold.

However, from my study of scripture which has been confirmed by many others, I have discovered that this mindset, though so popular, is a misrepresentation of the mind of God. Let me ask for instance, when did the 'going to heaven' agenda come into the picture? Was it before or after the fall? In other words, did pre-fallen Adam ever desire or pray to leave the earth and go to heaven? Did the bible ever suggest that, at some point, Adam and his wife would have been taken out of earth to heaven? If so, then who would have been left to manage God's earth? Would they have continued the creational mandate of procreation and replenishing the earth in heaven?

Perhaps not.

If so, we should then examine the other option, which is that going to heaven must have entered into God's mind after the fall. In other words, it was an after-thought. But that idea alone has far reaching implications that border on blasphemy: God is not all-knowing; and can be stopped from achieving His intent. Put elseway, God can fail – and the failure in this case is His inability to either prevent satan's interference or undo and remediate the mishap man's wrong choice wrought on His creation. Invariably, He is not that Almighty after all. The very idea that God needs to package a Plan B indirectly connotes the possibility of Him failing, Him being stoppable, and Him being finite in knowledge and power.

Yet what does the bible tell us?

> "I know that You can do all things, and that __no purpose of Yours can be thwarted__." —Job 42:2 [NASB]

That song I made reference to earlier tells us this much: He is too "old" to change; He is forever the same (Mal. 3:6). Even in human experience, the older a person gets, the more difficult it is to change. How much more the Ancient of Days. So, if Christianity as we know it is about escaping to heaven, would that not be an answer to satan's prayer – confine God to heaven while he, satan, can continues to hold sway on earth?

Restoration Is It

Much can still be said in this regard but we need to move on.

However, it should dawn on our hearts by now that we need to go back to the bible and rethink Christianity as a whole. Let us restate with greater emphasis: the centre focus of the scripture, of Christendom and every single activity we do therein should be restoration. But what do we have today? So many groups within Christendom have been defined by one scriptural emphasis or the other and each group wants its own particular emphasis to tower head and shoulder above all others.

But in them all, I have come to the personal conclusion that restoration is the all-encompassing program of God in this age of fallen man. As was pointed out earlier, it conveniently bridges all that God is doing in the immediate term, occasioned by the fall, to His overall ultimate intention. So, whatever your own branding within Christendom is, you ought to ask yourself: how is this an integral part of the restoration agenda?

If, for instance, you are into Discipleship, it must be within the context of God's program of restoration - otherwise you are doing your own thing. If you are into healing and deliverance or Word of Faith, or the Prayer movement or Missions or you are into the Holiness milieu, or the prophetic/apostolic bracket, or even the house church setting, all these must be in the context of restoration because they do not exist for their own self but are to lead us into the accomplishment of God's program of restoration.

Unfortunately, virtually all the various groups have somehow become 'stand-alone's and that has been the reason for the chaos in the Body, because once a group exists for itself and not within the framework of a larger Kingdom agenda, it becomes an end to itself and therefore disconnects from the whole counsel of God. It develops a competitive spirit and is threatened by other groups that emphasise something different. It reminds me of the parable that the Lord gave in Matt. 24:45-51 of the servant who forgot that he was to serve the Master's bidding, loses focus and begins to oppress his fellow servants and fool around.

What Exactly Is Restoration?

We have hammered so much on the word, restoration; So, what does it really mean? To start with, the use of the word "restoration" implies something must have been lost, stolen, damaged, deformed or subjected to wear and tear. What then, it may be asked, is that thing that needs be restored? The Kingdom of God – simple and straightforward.

Are we suggesting that the Kingdom of God ever got lost, stolen, damaged, deformed or subjected to wear and tear? Well, in a sense, the answer to that would be yes. To put it quite frankly, what happened in Eden was an overthrow. But let me give a background to this. Creation story started with the eternal Creator bringing forth His creation in two dimensions: the Invisible and the Visible; the Spiritual and the Physical; the Eternal and the Temporal; Heaven and Earth. And the influence, rule and sovereign power of God was administered in both domains/realms of creation.

Heaven, regarded as God's throne, is the headquarters and operational base of the invisible realm of creation while the earth is the headquarters and the operational base of the visible realm of creation. While God is directly in charge in heaven, He chose to administer His rule and dominion on earth through a regent, His proxy, created in His own image – corporate Man. Man's duty was to administer the government of God over all the earth in exactly the same way God governed in Heaven.

A simple analogy to clarify this point is to call to mind the way pre-independence Nigeria was run. It was the duty of the colonial administrator to ensure that as it was in Britain, so it is in Nigeria. Even though thousands of miles apart, the government was the same, the law and constitution were the same, the currency was the same; and through the process of western education, the culture and civilisation of the colonial power was brought to bear on the colony. Thus, Nigerians speak English, adopt English names, English clothing, diet and culture.

This was exactly the same relationship between Heaven and Earth. Man was God's colonial administrator on earth who administered the governance of heaven on the earth.

Consequences of the Fall

However, when man chose to obey the created rather than His Creator, a number of things ensued. Man lost the right of rule and became a subject to satan who took over the governance of the earth while the governance and the rule (Kingdom) of God became restricted to Heaven. That is why till date, the term 'the Kingdom of God' is often used to refer to heaven (especially because of Matthew's use of the term, "Kingdom of heaven"). This was not so until after the fall because, back then, the earth was as much the Kingdom of God as heaven. The earth manifested the glory, beauty, majesty, power and the order of God's Kingdom to the exact degree that heaven did. There was just no difference.

But after the fall, another operating system or a system of government took over the earth and began to recondition it in order to give expression to its own order of life (or civilisation). Thus, the perfect harmony that existed within creation got destroyed. This harmony is at five different levels:

— Harmony between God and man;
— Harmony between man and man;
— Harmony between man and creation;
— Harmony between creation and creation; and
— Harmony between God and creation.

Enmity followed; bitterness was rife and hostility became the order of the day. Further still, creation lost its ability to retain the knowledge of the glory of the Lord. What is the glory of the Lord? It is the beauty of the Lord. It is the exhibition of the gracefulness, the splendour, the dazzling beauty, the fragrance, the majesty, the supreme intelligence and ultimate wisdom of God.

However, let us note that even in man's fallen estate, the earth is still the Lord's (Psa. 24:1) and is filled with the glory of the Lord (Isaiah 6:2). The glory of the Lord in this context has much to do with the beauty, order and intelligence that are seen in God's creation – which was why the psalmist exclaimed in Psa. 8:1, *"Oh Lord our Lord, how excellent (majestic) is your name throughout all the earth!"* Paul alludes to this also in Rom. 1:20 – *"For since the creation of the world His invisible attributes, His eternal power and divine nature, have been clearly seen, being understood through what has been made, so that they are without excuse."* Unfortunately, however, man in his brutish fallen state often cannot perceive or comprehend (Psa. 92:5-6) and as a result, he is like a beast that perishes (Psa. 49:20)

Subsequently, man lost his original essence. He became like a wanderer lacking sense of purpose and divine direction (Pro. 21:16). And having lost his sense of purpose, he began to abuse his God-given endowments which are without repentance. His imagination and creativity became channelled to produce the worst forms of violence, unimaginable cruelty, lasciviousness, idolatry and orgies that led him farther away from his purpose and from his Creator.

These are some of the grim consequences of the fall – which is why I implied earlier that the administration of God's Kingdom on earth got lost and became restricted to heaven. However, God did not give up His creation; at no time did He surrender the ownership of His earth to satan. Even though satan had been accorded operational rights over the earth, God owns the absolute rights by virtue of He being the Creator. It is His sovereign power that still sustains the earth, that causes the sun to shine and the rain to fall as at when due, that causes the deer to calve and things of that nature. Satan is not in charge of all of that. He is the god of this world – but not the god of the earth.

The world, in the context of James 4:4 and 1 John 2:15-17, does not refer to the physical earth and the fullness thereof. Rather, it is like a virus which gained access into a computer, corrupted the original operating system and caused serious malfunctions of the hardware. The earth is the computer hardware, created, owned and loved by God. His Kingdom is the original operating system while the world is the virus introduced into the hardware that corrupted the O.S.

The good news is this: the virus will not remain in the hardware forever. The Creator had actually pre-empted this virus and had put up a long-term plan for restoration, and, in the process, would reveal several things about His divine personality which otherwise could not have been known or experienced. How else, for instance, would we have known Him as the Forgiver, Restorer and Redeemer, if no one had fallen? Thus, everything we see from Genesis 3 up to Revelations 20 is the unfolding of His restoration agenda. The restoration agenda is simply God's initiative to bring humanity back into its original estate as seen before the fall, in order for it to begin to fulfil its God-ordained intention for creation.

This is what Christianity is really about. That is why the singular message of Jesus was the reestablishment of the Kingdom on earth. The singular prayer He asked us to pray was *"Your Kingdom come, your will be done on earth as it is in Heaven"* (Matt. 6:10). Christianity is meant to promote the Kingdom agenda, epitomise the Kingdom philosophy, preach Kingdom message and express the Kingdom civilisation; Christianity without the

Kingdom is really another religion. We must strive to bring back the Kingdom into Christianity.

The Essence and the Structure

The Kingdom restoration agenda can be brought under two headlines: (1) Restoration of the Kingdom essence, and (ii) Restoration of the Kingdom structure.

I) Restoration of the Essence

What is meant by the essence? The simple dictionary meaning is the most important feature of a thing or the quality or nature of a thing that makes it what it is. For example, a chair is a chair as long as it serves the essence of being sat upon. If it gets broken in such a way that one can no longer sit on it, it has lost its essence and shouldn't really be called a chair anymore.

So, what is the essence of the Kingdom? What is the most important characteristic without which it cannot be said to be the Kingdom of God?

Owing to my Pentecostal background, I have always associated the Kingdom of God to the demonstration of supernatural power, ability to control nature at will and to go about with unquestionable authority. We often quote scriptures like, *"The Kingdom of God is not in word only but in power..."* While this of course is scripture, its interpretation, more often than not, is skewed and stretched beyond acceptable balance. Aside the fact that operating in the supernatural is not exclusive to us as Kingdom citizens, it is not the most important distinguishing factor of the Kingdom of God.

The word, kingdom, simply means the domain of the king. Obviously, the principal factor here is the king himself. What makes the kingdom is the person of the king himself - the totality of his person. His kingdom therefore is anywhere his personality commands submission. And his personality is a function of his nature. It is therefore in order to say that the Kingdom of God is anywhere His nature has been imbibed and is being given expression. The essential nature of God is love.

What is love? Love is not an emotional feeling of attraction. Love is not a strong desire for or attraction to something or someone. Love is a principle, a nature, a philosophy of life that puts others first. Love is that attitude to life that prefers to go down so that others can go up. Love does not think of self, first. It is voluntary, unconditional sacrificial commitment. Love is selfless. True love is of God, for God is love.

The attributes of love are recorded in I Cor. 13 and in Gal. 5:22,23. Love is patient; love is kind; love is not arrogant or puffed up; love does not flaunt himself; love is not vengeful; love does not insist on its own; love is not malicious. You can't be manifesting any of these attributes and claim you are walking in love. In fact, going by the words of the beloved apostle, John, you can't even claim you know God.

The Kingdom of God is therefore a whole system of life that is cultured and constituted by this principle of love. It is sad that this is not emphasised in Christianity as we know it. It is not our focus in our churches and ministries today. At best, it is merely a sermon preached during wedding ceremonies. We would rather focus on our religious activities, which are merely the externalities; more often than not, the internal motivation of those activities is something other than genuine selfless love for God and for humanity.

The restoration agenda will however focus on bringing back the Kingdom essence into Christendom. This will be done as God raises teachers and leaders who will teach with divine illumination and authority the message of the Kingdom of God in its correct context and application. As they teach, much emphasis will equally be given to Kingdom lifestyle development. Let me say that what will actually bring the unbelieving world to its knees is not our ability to heal the sick and raise the dead but our ability to walk in love towards one another, towards even the unlovable.

ii) Restoration of Structure

A structure is a set arrangement put in place in order to sustain a system. A structure does not exist for itself; it is meant to enable or support a given function. In this context, a house is a structure but shelter is the essence. A wedding ceremony is a structure; the marriage is the essence. The school system is a structure; education is the essence. The judiciary and law-enforcements are structures; maintaining justice and social order is the essence.

Structures are inevitable; even creation itself is a structure put in place by God to give expression to His greatness and awesome majesty. The Garden of Eden was another structure God planted and placed man therein. A system is only as good and effective as the structures put in place.

For any activity to be sustained, for any purpose to be realised, for the smooth running of our lives and society, structures are needed. In fact, like the examples given earlier, human life and society revolve round structures. Structures are directly related to the essence (function). If the structure is not right, the essence (purpose) can never be realized.

It is therefore very absurd for anyone to think that the structure is unimportant; I have often heard people say that we only need to emphasise the spirit. What a laugh. The spirit without the structure is nothing. It brings to mind many great and highly anointed servants of God who died prematurely because they overworked their bodies (the structure that houses their spirits).

In my study of the Assembly life viz-a-viz human society, I was able to identify some major structures that we have to relate with:

1. Structures of doctrine (our belief system)
2. Structures of settlements (fellowship)
3. Structures of leadership
4. Structures of finance
5. Structures of ministry

For the purpose of this study, we shall limit ourselves to the structure of settlements – which is where we find the structure of the family.

CHAPTER TWO

KEY INPUTS OF THE FAMILY IN THE BIBLICAL STORYLINE

The Bible - God's Story of Restoration

That the bible is all-time's greatest bestseller is unarguable; no empirical research is required to substantiate this claim. Since the invention of the printing press almost 600 years ago, about 5 billion copies of the bible has been printed in hundreds of versions and in 2,000 different languages of the world - and still counting! In some field of study, the bible is actually a recommended text for literature. Written over a span of about 1,500years in which over 50 writers had inputs, it could have taken no less than the deliberate orchestration of the Supreme Intelligence to weave this several hundreds of stories through a spectrum of time into one perfect masterpiece of literature.

In this one book, there is poetry, history, letters, songs, anecdotes and all branches of literature you can ever think of. They however do have one single focal point or storyline which is the essence of scripture. Growing up as children, whenever we read any novel or watched any movie, the first thing we were encouraged to figure out is the storyline. In all these various weaves and plots, what does the author have in mind? What story is he trying to form for me to see?

Similarly, the bible has a very unambiguous storyline. It tells the story of God's relationship with humanity - a story of love, betrayal, forgiveness, redemption, reconciliation and ultimately restoration. In it, we see the beauty and harmony of God's world which was later destroyed by the introduction of sin and disobedience. We then see God spelling out His agenda for restoration.

The bible has two main divisions namely the Old Testament (O.T) and the New Testament (N.T). The O.T is like an allegorical representation of God's unfolding plan of redemption, reconciliation and restoration. Everything we see in the O.T is God's way of telling not just the story of *His own way* of bringing mankind back into union with Himself (reconciliation) consequent upon that Edenic tragedy but *His own idea* of how humanity should have existed (original design) had the fall never happened.

Let us put it this way to help our understanding. Today, human society runs on various sectors such as the political, economic, social, health, education, judicial systems and so on. Think of this for a moment: had the fall never happened, would we be running the health system or the judicial system the way we currently do? The obvious answer is no. Why? Because the current systems have been conditioned by the fact of the fall.

In that case, how then should these various systems have been run had the fall never happened? Think about how Adam's family would have looked like assuming the fall never happened; and in a fully restored earth when, finally, the Kingdom is firmly established, how do you think families on earth will be run? This is the goal of restoration; this is what the

Lord meant when He asked us to pray: *"Your will be done on earth as it is in heaven."*

Thus, stories in the O.T. like God calling out Abraham and making of Him a nation are not just for building ethical values but are all prophetic shadows that when accurately decoded, reveal clearly God's own idea regarding human life and cohabitation.

We need to say this for the umpteenth time, this is actually the essence of Christianity: to engage actively in modelling God's idea for the rest of the world to see – just like the physical nation of Israel in the O.T was God's model to the rest of the heathen nations to showcase His own idea of how human life and society ought to be constituted.

A Picture of a Restored Earth

To leave us in no doubt regarding the centre stage the Kingdom message occupies in the biblical storyline, the Author in His literary prowess ensured that both testaments give a clear picture of the endgame: an earth in which the Kingdom has become fully restored. In the O.T., we see snapshots of this clearly in passages like Isaiah 11:1-9; 33:20-24; 65:17-25; in Micah 4:1-4 and in Zechariah 8:3-5 – among other prophetic scriptures. Painted for us is the scenario of a new heaven and earth wherein there is peace, mutual respect and harmony. Similarly, in the N.T, we see this clearly in Revelations 21 & 22. This is to make it elaborately clear that God is in the business of restoration.

So, how does the family come into the picture? Does the family have any role to play in bringing this glorious vision to pass? Certainly, it does. To see how, first take time to carefully read through the scriptures suggested earlier which all portray the Kingdom age; and then pause to think for a moment: what comes into your mind when you think about Heaven or paradise? I am sure you will think of an egalitarian society; a place of bliss, perfect harmony, love, sharing, a utopia. You will visualise children playing around, and animals lying down peacefully, undisturbed. At the very heart of that picture is the family; the family is the unit of any society. It is impossible to talk about human life and co-existence without talking of the family. Thus, at the heart of the restoration agenda is the family.

Let us now highlight the different times the family structure featured prominently in God's storyline both in the O.T and N.T with a view to decoding their meaning and relevance to the restoration agenda.

Flashpoints of the Family in the O.T.

1. The family was right there in Genesis when God Himself planted the garden which was to serve as man's home.

2. Noah's family was instrumental to the preservation of the human race.

3. After the flood, the division of the earth was by language and family - Gen 10:5.

4. God's covenant with Abram – "*…through you and your seed shall all the families of the earth be blessed*" - was in a family context. That word, seed, actually means lineage or family line. The same applies to, "*Your seed shall possess the gates of the enemy*".

5. It was a family that went into Egypt; that stayed there for 430years after which it took the Lord's strong hand to bring them out.

6. The Passover, an ordinance which was very critical to their emancipation was to be observed family by family. In fact, anyone who didn't have a family of his own must join one family unit, and anyone caught loafing around outside the covering of a household did not live to tell the story.

Interesting isn't it? This ordinance did not recognise nationality; only the blood on households. In other words, a bonafide Hebrew caught outside the household was killed but an Egyptian who comes under the covering of the household was spared.

7. In the wilderness, God seemed to relate with them family by family. That is why if somebody was to be mentioned, the scriptures would trace his genealogy - from the whole nation under God to his tribe, from tribe to clan and from clan down to the family. Each family had its head as well as clans and tribes. We saw this vividly when they wanted to deal with sin in the camp (the Achan episode).

8. Judgment came not only on Korah and his colleagues but on their entire households as well. Same with Achan.

9. The arrangement (settlements) of the nation around the tabernacle was by families and tribes.

10. We note that God's instructions came to a family setting in Gen. 1; and when error came in, it was through a family. All instructions given to the Israelites right from their period of leaving Egypt through the wilderness to the period of Joshua were to be implemented at family levels. Thus, any instruction or divine truth that has not been received and worked out at the family level will remain a bogus concept. It is important therefore to strive to bring these kingdom truths to families for them to begin to walk in.

This is why it is very important to have a fully functioning unit where the parents are pastors to nurture their household in the way of truth. They are to help themselves and their children to walk accurately in the principles of the Spirit. John the Apostle commended the elect lady because he found her children walking in the truth. God's mandate to Abraham highlighted this responsibility very clearly (Gen. 18:19). It is important to note that the reason God called Abraham was not for him to raise a mighty army for Him or build Him a mega city; instead it was for him to instruct his children in the way of justice and judgment.

11. When the patriarchs (Jacob and Moses) were to pronounce the patriarchal blessing, it was pronounced family by family.

12. It was at the family level that understandings regarding God's dealing with them as a people were passed down to their offspring. (Exod. 12:25-27, Joshua 4:6,7, Psa. 78:5-7)

13. It was also at the family level that sons were dedicated onto the Lord's service. In fact, it was a shame for any family not to have any of their sons given to the Lord.

14. Returning from captivity, they took time to reinstate family lines, clan lines and tribal lines.

15. In Joel, the end-time prophecy: *"In the last days, I will pour out my spirit upon all flesh: <u>sons</u> and <u>daughters</u> will prophesy, <u>young men</u> will see visions, <u>old men</u> will dream dreams; even upon the <u>housemaids and menservants</u>"* (Joel 2:28-29) was in the context of households/families.

16. In Zechariah 14 where the picture of a restored earth is described, it says the families of the earth will go to Jerusalem yearly to worship and the family that fails to go to worship, onto them shall there not be rain (vs. 17). Here, nations are addressed as families, buttressing the fact that the use of families in Gen. 12 is also in the context of nations i.e. in you and your seed shall all the families (nations) of the earth be blessed. We also see this in Amos 3:2 *"You only have I chosen among all the families of the earth..."* (NASB). In Isa. 33:20, Jerusalem is described as "a quiet home".

17. Talking about restoration, when we see the picture of paradise (or a restored earth) in Zechariah 8 or Psalm 144, we see clearly, a picture of community i.e. a network of close-knit families. This is what is alluded to in Psalm 133. And of

course, God made His arrangement known to Abraham in saying, *"In you and your seed shall all the families of the earth be blessed"*.

This clearly means that when God looks into the earth, what He desires to see are families spread throughout the face of the earth in peaceful harmonious co-existence. When we see nations, God sees families. In God's viewpoint, geo-political entities we refer today as nations are not as important as the family, as can be implied from the Passover episode wherein nationality was not a factor. The family therefore is the foundation of any nation. Save a family and you have saved a nation; change a family and you have changed a nation; destroy a family and you have destroyed the nation. This informs my maxim: the love of money is not really the root of all evil but a bad marriage.

To buttress this further, we notice the consistent use of the term, "House of Israel" in the O.T. This is so as to drum it into the consciousness of the people that they were a family. "House of Israel" appears in the scriptures 152 times; "house of Judah" occurs 40 times; "house of the Lord" occurs 232 times. Not only has the Lord chosen to designate His nation as a House, He also chose to designate the community of those who have sworn allegiance to Christ as His (Christ's) house. (Eph. 2:19-21; Heb. 3:5,6; 10:19-21).

Here are a few more scriptures to show the family as relevant to divine agenda:

> *Therefore, you shall lay up these words of mine in your heart and in your soul, and bind them as a sign on your hand, and they shall be as frontlets between your eyes. <u>You shall teach them to your children, speaking of them when you sit in your house,</u> when you walk by the way, when you lie down, and when you rise up. And <u>you shall write them on the doorposts of your house and on your gates,</u> that <u>your days and the days of your children</u>*

may be multiplied in the land of which the Lord swore to your fathers to give them, like the days of the heavens above the earth. —Deut. 11:18-21

Then the Lord will create above every dwelling place of Mount Zion, and above her assemblies, a cloud and smoke by day and the shining of a flaming fire by night. For over all the glory there will be a covering. —Isaiah 4:5

"At the same time," says the LORD, "I will be the God of all the families of Israel, and they shall be My people." —Jer. 31:1

The reason for pointing out these scriptures is for us to realise that the idea of family is more than what we are made to believe when contracting the vows. We think it in terms of an obligation to give expression to our own human cravings for sex, companionship and procreation. But these are only a secondary objective; the primary objective is to be the cradle of God's civilisation. When the table is turned and the secondary is made the main focus, the family becomes an idol and therefore an enemy to God's purpose. Little wonder it has brought forth all forms of chaos and conflicts. We will see more of this in the next chapter.

Before we go on to examine the inputs of the family arrangement in the N.T., let us pause and examine, in the next chapter, one of the most fundamental issues regarding marriage and the family.

CHAPTER THREE

THE FAMILY - GOD'S IDEA

A Kingdom Perspective to the Essence of the Family

In the Introduction, we pointed out the obvious: families are hurting, marriages are collapsing, Christian couples are soiling their testimony and these are not good for our Christian witness. To address this, different ministries focusing on marriage and the family have risen in the Body of Christ; marriage seminars are organised; marriage committees are set up in churches to counsel both intending and existing couples; books are written – all to help couples in handling the challenges that come up in the family and arrest the ugly trend of breakdown of the famil0y.

Purpose X-Rayed

In spite of all these laudable efforts however, there seem to be no respite to this social anomaly. Rather, they seem to be on the increase. Why? What are we not doing well? We cited the common saying much earlier in the book: purpose not known, abuse inevitable. Could it be that all our efforts are like dealing with the branches instead of addressing a more fundamental issue which is our understanding of the true essence of the family? These were my ponderings when, at a time, I became increasingly dissatisfied with the popular reasons for marriage read out in most wedding services, given below:

1.   Companionship,
2.   Procreation, and
3.   (Sexual) satisfaction

A deeper reflection on these three reveals a simple fact: they are all centred on self. If marriage is all about this, then it is essentially for man, by man and of man: so how is God glorified in this arrangement since ALL THINGS were made and must be for His pleasure (Rev. 4:11)? To start with the first reason, companionship, has it ever occurred to you that the first man never complained about being alone or needing a companion? It was entirely God's idea and that was why it was so convenient for the man to push it back on Him when the chips were down. As far as it rested with him, he was doing just fine.

Let us also take note that procreation does not necessarily have to be through sexual reproduction. After all, Eve did not come forth that way. If marriage and family is all about reproduction, don't think it is impossible for the All-powerful God to cause mankind to reproduce asexually, just as it with is with some plants and lower animal species.

We do not know how long the pre-fall period in the Garden lasted but I can place a wager that the first couple did not think of sex until after the fall. In my wild thinking, if they had copulated, the amount of life they carried in their pre-fallen estate would have caused Eve to take in at the very first blow. And, needless to say, in immortality, there is no copulation.

If sexual intercourse with your spouse is a way of pleasing God, I wonder why there is no arrangement for that in eternity. If breeding young is what causes God to be glorified, then this should actually continue on a larger scale in heaven. And if the hallmark of companionship is marriage, then companionship does not exist in Heaven!

Questionable Foundations

Why this line of argument? What are we driving at? Very simple: the marriage system as we know it today is built on questionable foundations. That is why crises erupt anytime anyone of these assumptions is missing in the family. That is why a couple will feel unfulfilled if they do not have any issue and this can threaten whatever happiness and commitment they have to each other. There are several cases of pastors having a second wife because, according to them, their first wife could not produce any offspring for them. As far as such pastors are concerned, marriage is all about childbearing; after all, the bible says, *"Be fruitful and multiply..."* So, when the rubber touches the road, the talk of weathering the storms together flies out the window.

That is why some sisters would keep a secret affair to service their passion for sex, having found out (after the wedding night) that their hubby can't perform (and if they are not audacious enough to pull out of the relationship). "Why, he wasn't fair to me!" she would justify herself in her heart. "Why didn't he tell me before we got married?" While not holding brief for such a man, my sister, I thought you loved him! So, what you loved is really not him but your own desire for those three objectives. And this brings us right back to the definition of love. Most of us are in relationship not out of bible love but selfish desire.

Looking at it from this angle, it becomes so clear that a lot of the marriage crises we try to resolve (and some defy our solutions and the inevitable ensues) revolves around these three human needs. And that is just what they are - human needs.

Marriage is Covenant

Lest I be misunderstood, the examples I gave above do not imply that I justify acts of irresponsibility such as concealing such a vital information from your would-be spouse. I only used those examples to expose the real reason many go into the relationship without realizing one fundamental truth which I state in the words of Barrister Emeka Nwankpa: **Marriage is covenant and covenant is marriage** - full stop. We simply cannot overemphasise this. Any covenant we see in scriptures is marriage - whether between God and man, man and the devil or man and man. Can we be brutally honest: it has very little to do with compatibility, likeness, convenience and so on. Once a covenant is entered into, ignorance is no excuse.

An appropriate reference for this is the covenant that Joshua entered into with the Gibeonites. God's perfect will was for Joshua to wipe out the inhabitants of the land and that was what Joshua was committed to doing. But these fellows somehow outwitted Joshua and God! Once they struck the covenant, even God had to honour it to the extent that about 400 years later, when Saul violated that covenant, God Himself rose up to deal with the breach.

So, at a point in my journey, I became thoroughly convinced that there has to be more about the family than merely meeting these human needs, important as they are. Again, my conviction stems from the fact that everything must be for His pleasure. And so, the family is first and foremost to serve God's interest; our own enjoyment and fulfilment are derivatives of that. In view of this, I began to search deep down within to see if there is any other more God-centred reason in which the Kingdom derives greater benefit. I made two discoveries which will take us back into Genesis.

Work for Man to Do

First of all, I found out that the reason God made the helpmeet for the man was not so that they could just have fun, be happy and swim in abundance and absolute freedom – which is what the popular fairy-tale thinking makes us believe. Rather, it was so that man could be more effective in the work that had been committed to his hands. If it was about enjoying companionship and all, then God should have created them at the same time. But notice that man had assumed duty a good while before His Employer reasoned within Himself that even though he was doing a great job (so Adam must have thought), it didn't meet His expectations and therefore needed help. Take note that Adam wasn't consulted in this whole setup; it was not about Adam; neither was it about the woman.

From the onset, the woman being brought into the scene must have known that she had a divine obligation to fulfil. So it would be a serious omission for the duo to lose sight of the divine assignment and start focusing on themselves and the perks that came along with their mandate.

Now, can we ask ourselves: how many parties are involved in the marriage covenant? Based on the popular understanding, many will say two, of course: the man and the woman. But in the light of what we have just shared, how many parties are really involved in this arrangement we now refer to as marriage? Three; the covenant of marriage is not just between man and the woman but between man, woman and the Initiator of marriage - God. Marriage is a covenant arrangement that brings a man and woman together in partnership with God. It is two people agreeing to work together with God.

So in thinking about the essence for bringing the duo together, we must do away with the fairy-tale mentality of two naked couples just having fun in a garden; we must develop the notion that they were brought into a position of assuming responsibility; they were brought into partnership with a Senior partner who in every respect has been introduced throughout scripture as a Worker. Take away the divine mandate from any marriage and it becomes another dysfunctionality, no matter how well they lived together and brought forth many children.

What then is that divine mandate man was called to do which he couldn't do effectively without a partner? Now, this is the most critical part of this chapter. Quite naturally, if somebody is not measuring up, the first think one thinks of is capacity building: send him for a few training programs. Capacity building in the spiritual context could be a release of an anointing. But in God's wisdom, that would not suffice. There was something in the job description which would be impossible for Adam to do quite effectively without a complete human being like himself.

But in providing an able assistant, why not a fellow man, a younger brother to Adam you might think? Why a creature with a completely different physiological and psychological framework? It was like the divine arrangement was set out to fail from the start because to work together, would you not need two people who have similar configurations in order to function harmoniously?

So, what exactly is the nature of this work? Again, I hope you will not start thinking of tending a nice garden and becoming a baby factory. It's much more than that.

To find answers to these questions, we need to go back to Genesis.

God as Community/Marriage of Spirits

Then God said, "Let Us make man in Our image, according to Our likeness; let them have dominion over the fish of the sea, over the birds of the air, and over the cattle, over all the earth and over every creeping thing that creeps on the earth." —Gen. 1:26

This verse opens with God saying, *"Let Us"*. Who exactly was He speaking to? To start with, He wasn't talking to angels as some have erroneously perceived. No; angels are not in God's image and likeness. It has to be something else.

Okay, so was He speaking to other Gods? After all, the very word, "God" introduced in Gen. 1:1, and in almost throughout scripture, is translated from the Hebrew text, *Elohim*, which is translated literally as Creators – a plural. Does it not connote the idea of plural Gods? That certainly cannot be, *"…For there is one God; and there is no other but He…"* (Mark 12:32). How then do we solve this riddle?

Increasingly, I am beginning to see God as not just a unitary Being but an institution; a community – similar to "the Presidency". The Presidency is not just Mr. President but an entire parastatal with different personnel, offices, departments and agencies. To clarify further, think of the Nigerian Senate. The Senate is not just a single person but an organ in the legislative arm of government. It comprises many senators with the Senate president being first among equals. And whenever the Senate passes a resolution on a matter and makes it public, it is not the person or even office of the Senate President that has spoken but the entire Senate as an organ of government.

In the same vein, when the bible reads, *"And God said, let us…"*, it wasn't as if one God was speaking to other Gods, it was a resolution that was reached within the community of the Godhead. However, the best analogy the Lord has used to teach me about the God community is water. Everybody knows that water is just water; it is an uncountable noun. Yet, elementary science lets us know that water is not an element but a compound, formed when three elements come together: two atoms of hydrogen and one atom of oxygen.

Now, oxygen by itself is not water; ditto for hydrogen. Yet, when these three uniquely distinct elements combine together, they form a completely new product that could not have been if one of the elements is absent in the equation. And despite the fact that this new product is as a result of the marriage of three elements, nobody questions the "oneness" of water. In the same way, who all creation knows as God (the Creator) is the combination of three distinct "elements" in an eternal accord or bonding, call it marriage. Hence, the very concept of God connotes a marriage or a bonding or a fellowship (communion) of spirits. And it was that marriage that brought forth creation as we know it. In that singular statement, *"Let us make man in our own image"*, we see the Will, the Force (power, energy, life, ability etc.) and the Form all at play.

Now, it is the nature of all spirits to express. Oh, how spirits love to express themselves and until they do so, they feel caged. But to do so, they need a material, a space, a world, a body as the medium of expression. So, God, the Father of all spirits, in His wisdom and according to His eternal plan, brought forth creation to showcase the rich and vast variety that exists within Himself i.e. the God community. That is the crucial work the man was created to engage in. The male species, all by himself couldn't have expressed this dimension (the bonding or fellowship within the God-community) without a counterpart.

Thus, man(kind) was also made to be an institution, a community of two unique and distinct varieties – male and female – in order to express the same life that sustains the God community and keeps them one – what great mystery! Think about it: what keeps water from falling apart back into its individual components? What keeps these components so fitly integrated together that, in water, they have completely lost their individual identities and are content with being expressed in the corporate reality? There is a bonding; a fellowship; an accord –

and Man was made to very visibly demonstrate that fellowship. That is what it means to be made in God's image.

In other words, when God looks at humankind, He wants to see Himself. Humankind, therefore, is a mirror (thus, the word, image) to reflect God back to Himself. The God/Kingdom civilisation is that which expresses the sweet harmony of the marriage of Spirits. Whenever that harmony is given expression, life, which is the order of the Kingdom, ensues. The principle that gives birth to that harmony (shared life or community) is called love.

The Foundation is Love

The opposite of love however is self. The principle of self is the foundation for and the driving force/energy behind the divorce or disharmony of (between) spirits. And when self is given expression in contrast to love, disharmony (otherwise called death) ensues. And death has since reigned over all creation since the fall. Man, now ruled by self-interests, tries co-habiting with others who are in the same boat of self-rule; do you see how inevitable it is for interpersonal conflicts to arise? As a matter of fact, all human misery stems from this post-fall nature of man: me at your expense.

The family is however a union between two established on the foundation of that which is the opposite of self: love. Without this foundation, you can as well forget the family. What is love? Though we have touched on this earlier, this matter cannot be overemphasised. Please, just throw away completely the Hollywood definition of love. In fact, love is one of the most abused words in human language. It is an abuse of the word, for instance to say, "I love mangoes." When a guy looks at a lady and says, "I love you", 99% of the time, he only means to say, "I need you to satisfy a human need." In other words, it is himself who he actually loves.

The Kingdom definition for love is willingness to die for the other to live; to serve the other; to bend over backwards for the sake of the other. Love is asking the question, what can I give? It is not asking, "What is in it for me" but "How can I serve the interest of the other?" It is not about how the other can serve one's own interest.

To establish this from scriptures, let us check a few bible passages:

> For God so loved the world that He gave His only begotten Son... — John 3:16
>
> Greater love has no one than this, than to lay down one's life for his friends. — John 15:13
>
> By this we know love, because He laid down His life for us. And we also ought to lay down our lives for the brethren. — 1 John 3:16

In plain words, love in God's sight is laying down one's life. In view of this, the fellow who enjoys eating mangoes doesn't love the mangoes but loves himself. All expressions of love in the earth are actually a love of self. So, when a person gets to a marriageable age; it is that same love for self that drives him/her to look for a companion because it is a plain human need, further compounded by societal pressure.

Mark my word, there is no marriage that is entered into with that self-motive that will last. It is only a matter of time, it will collapse. Actually, some have internally collapsed for long; it has only not manifested on the outside. The same applies to every form of relationship: business partnership – you name it. Self will ALWAYS engender division, scattering, hostility, separation and death.

So, God instituted marriage because He himself is a marriage. Man was called to give expression to that marriage. The family is the smallest unit of human co-habitation. Every family built and runs on the principle of love and shared life is actually fulfilling the real God-reason for marriage. The shared life operated at family level is also carried on into inter-family (communal) relationships and spreads outwards till the whole earth is filled with a glorious picture of mankind in harmony. That was what God wanted to see, not just animals, vegetation and the earth's crust. He wants to see the whole earth covered with humankind living His life. When this happens, the man(kind) is expressing God's image and likeness.

God Hates Divorce

That is why God hates divorce. Divorce is an expression of the refusal to subscribe to shared life, God's way of life. When a couple files for divorce, they are saying in essence that they cannot cohabit with each other based on the principle of love i.e. how things were before the fall, how things are in heaven right now; and how things will be in a restored earth. The family system is a real acid test for anybody who professes they are walking in love.

You can claim to love a brother or sister who you see only once or twice a week in church or you work together from 8am to 4pm. But it is only because you have not come close to such an individual to live under the same roof in a family arrangement. So as far as I John 4:20 is concerned, how much you really love God (or any human being for that matter) can be measured by how much you walk in love towards the members of your family.

No wonder the scriptures teaches that any man who is not able to live out the principle of the Kingdom (which is summed up under the word, love) within the structure of his family essentially has no message. The admonition the scripture seems to have for any man whose marriage is in a mess and yet aspiring to work for God is: Go set your house in order first, you have no message or ministry till you do so.

We have seen cases of brothers acting so nice to other church members or colleagues, going the extra mile to help them, yet these same brothers cannot show the same level of kindness to their spouses at home. We have seen sisters acting so meek and humble to other men outside the home but are just not able to express the same level of deference and submission to their husbands at home. The simple reason for this is that they can put up an act for a few hours of the day but there is no room for acting in the family. And as such, many believers carry on in duality. This is why Wolfgang Simson surmised that the most difficult place to put up an act is in the home.

Marriage Not About Compatibility

In the modern world, compatibility probably ranks the highest in the list of considerations when deciding for marriage. However, I strongly believe that marriage is not really about compatibility. Before you raise your objection, remember that among our ancestors, it was not really an issue they talked about. In fact, their parents made choices for them and they simply complied. And those marriages lasted far longer than contemporary times in which we burn so much energy over compatibility.

The whole subject of compatibility arises simply because we have not departed from the "self" principle. And as long as we still take it at that level, the true essence of marriage (showcasing an order of life wherein the parties are laying down their individual lives for one another) is still being defeated. It only means we are trying to match two likeable persons together while we put at arm's length those who are 'not compatible' with us. Well, the implication of that is we are conceding to the fact that in this realm of life, the "self" principle is king and cannot be brought to its knees in surrender to the supremacy of the life of God in Christ.

All relationships, marriage and the family most of all, create a platform for us to come together with entirely different individuals to give expression to the God's kind of life. So the family according to God's original design is God's structure that facilitates learning the principle of walking in love/shared life in order to be integrated into the larger community of mankind. Here, we learn the language, the culture and the values of the Kingdom. Akin to the natural order, we start as babblers/toddlers and progress steadily till we can fully communicate and walk in that order of life.

CHAPTER FOUR

THE FAMILY IN NEW TESTAMENT ASSEMBLY LIFE AND PRACTICE

In Chapter Two, we highlighted the inputs of the family in the Old Testament. From that study, we discovered that the family structure has played a very significant role in the restoration blueprint which is what the O.T actually is. We saw that the family formation was paramount in averting judgment, bringing salvation, in preserving divine processes, in recruiting and discipling entire generations, in communicating instructions and so on.

In this chapter, we want to look at the place of the family in the New Testament assembly life and practice.

Flashpoints of the Family in the N.T

1. In Acts 2:46; 5:42; 20:20, they met and taught from house to house.

2. In Acts 8:3, Paul entered "every house"- a clear reference to households where Christians gathered for devotion and fellowship (we call them churches today). Also check Rom. 16:5, 1 Cor. 16:19, Col. 4:15, Philemon :2.

56

3. In Acts 16, Paul said, *"Believe on the Lord and you will be saved and your household"*. In other words, crucial decisions as per the faith, the embrace of truth etc. were done at family levels, corroborating what we saw in the O.T.

4. In Titus, Paul accused some of subverting households – another clear reference to the Ekklesia-in-the-family arrangement. These households were more than just a nuclear family but a home assembly

5. John the Apostle commended the elect lady because he found her children walking in the truth.

From these references, it is clear that the family arrangement was what the pioneer Christian Assembly depended on for growth, sustenance and discipleship.

World over, whenever reference is made to what can be called the most ideal picture of the body of believers throughout history, the Ekklesia of the first century (early church) has always been the reference point. Why? It has to be more than the miracles because miracles have always happened even up till now. Reading Acts 2:41-45 and Acts 4:32-35, I had to conclude that it has to do with the life, the love, the warmth, the fellowship, the togetherness, the transparency, the brotherhood – all which defied all human logic as these people were not related by biology and only family ties could have ever produced such strong commitment to one another.

The Family Structure - The Secret

So, what structure facilitated this strong bonding? Remember that we defined structure in Chapter One as an arrangement put in place to support a function. From the account of the Assembly life documented in the N.T (which we have seen from above), the following facts are obvious:

1. Believers met from house to house.

2. The family was at the centre of assembly life and activities. True, they met in the early years at Solomon's porch to receive apostolic doctrine but it was at the family level that those teachings were broken down, bread was broken and real communal life of the Body was expressed.

3. The Christian family/household was more than a nucleus of father, mother and children – a biological unit; it was a mini-community that transcended biology. Here, they were learning to know no man after the flesh. It was a place of integration, grooming and discipleship. It was a local assembly.

4. Because Ekklesia was expressed in homes, the Body of Christ functioned more like a family than an organization. Everything about the Assembly was organic. They did not run "services" where any Dick Tom and Harry can simply walk in for a religious feel. In fact, Ekklesia was not a meeting people go to but a life that they live.

Today, the family is no more the centre of Assembly life but the church building and Christian organizations. Back then, the word, Ekklesia, was a collective that was always used in reference to the body of believers and never a building or any organisation.

Back then, the breakdown of the Ekklesia looks like this:

- The Christian home (the smallest unit of the Assembly)
- The Assembly in the neighbourhood (probably made up of 3 or 4 families)
- The Assembly in a local area (probably made up of 2 or 3 neighbourhood assemblies)
- The Assembly in the city (a collective of all the neighbourhood assemblies in the city)

A believer of the first century would be shocked to hear of a St.

Paul's church or a St. Peter's cathedral as we have today. Back then, no one would ask questions like: "You're a member of what church?" Brethren simply gathered in the home closest to them or they made their homes available for other saints to gather organically. Today, the term, 'local assembly' has become complex organisations of men.

Advantages of the First Century Pattern of Home Assemblies

We have seen that the structure of the Ekklesia back then was purely based on households/families. What are the advantages of this?

1. Ekklesia is closest to where people live, and as such, believers are completely at home with one another. With the present arrangement of 'going to church', it is easy for hypocrisy to thrive.

2. The simplicity of Assembly life is preserved here. Bureaucracy, formality, hierarchy, organization are all at the barest minimum.

3. Because of the moderate size, believers know one another; there is no room for hiding. Intimacy and brotherhood are strongest here.

4. Because of its moderate size, authentic fellowship is made possible. The word fellowship comes from the Greek word, *koinonia,* which means: participate, communicate, contribute, distribute, interact. All these words require active involvement on the part of everyone in the *koinonia*. Without meaning to cast aspersions on church organizations, true fellowship cannot hold where there is a crowd, and this crowd is the dream of every present-day pastor.

5. Hero worship, one-man superstar syndrome, "church" built round one man or his family cannot survive.

6. Because it is not about one man and his gifting, the headship, centrality and pre-eminence of Christ is better expressed.

7. There is greater opportunity for the practical implementation of the priesthood of all believers where saints are free to express their God-allocated graces. The culture of *"One-Anothering"* is fostered among brethren.

8. The demand on people to live right is strongest.

9. Evangelism is strongest this way.

10. Running "church" will be at very minimal cost. Today, church business is capital intensive.

11. Unity among believers is maintained while division and denominationalism can hardly thrive.

12. It is almost impossible for one home assembly to have so much and another assembly not to have at all, since they were not building upwards but spreading outwards.

Let me make an important caveat here: all too often in history, we have seen believers make certain forms or patterns the focus such that others then attempt to replicate the form without the life. The form is nothing in itself without the life. Therefore, the life should be our greatest priority. Secondly, the concept of home assemblies is more than just brethren gathering inside someone's living room; it is possible to gather in a living room with a cathedral mentality and practices. There is much to be said in this regard, which will be the subject for another book.

Furthermore, home assemblies as presented in this book is not the same thing as house/cell fellowships run by many churches today. The latter, obviously, is connected to - and is under the administration of - a parent church. In most cases, outlines have been prepared and there is a designated cell leader to coordinate things as structured by the parent body. In short, it is a scaled down version of the parent church. More often than not, it is the members of the parent church that constitutes 95% of those who attend these cell fellowships.

A Pattern For Us

We have taken time to look at both the Old and the New Testaments to point out two things: one, the Assembly in homes is not just a New Testament idea but as old as the bible. Two, it is often argued that the Home Assembly arrangement was the only option available to the first century Christians because of persecution. So they couldn't meet in public buildings or own property.

This is totally untrue. Let us remember that despite the persecution, the pioneer Christian Assembly waxed stronger. And what's more, most of these early Christians were Jews who were already grounded in the culture of building synagogues wherever they found themselves. So, if Christianity of the early times was synagogue-centred and driven as we have today, against all odds, they still would have built their own version of synagogues or temple.

It is also touted that back then, Christians were still very few, unlike what we have today where we number in millions. Again, this is not an issue at all. There were big and metropolitan cities like Rome and Ephesus back then where literally thousands of believers resided. But because they had no denominational mindset, they simply spread outwards such that more home assemblies were being formed every day as more people came into the faith.

Things however started to degenerate when the fellowship of believers moved out of the family formation into buildings. Again, this is inevitable, because when we assume we can tamper with certain foundational patterns, we jeopardise the integrity of the entire structure. I think David just assumed he could bring in some good ideas into the way the Ark is carried; he later realised his error and returned to the due order. Oh that God's people would rise up and return to the due order.

I'll use the words of Witness Lee to drive home the very vital point to note here:

> "There are many Christians who ... believe that the practice of the Assembly as revealed in the New Testament is merely a historical antecedent, not a norm for Assembly practice in the present day. However, there are a minority of Christians who have seen that THE NEW TESTAMENT REVELATION OF THE EKKLESIA IS NOT ONLY HISTORICAL, BUT ALSO NORMATIVE, THAT IS, IT IS INTENDED TO GOVERN THE PRACTICE OF THE ASSEMBLY LIFE IN THIS (and every) GENERATION.
>
> Regarding the Ekklesia, God has not left us to our own opinion. His way is made known in His Word. Just as the revelation of the Scripture is normative concerning the gospel, salvation, and the proper Christian life, so it is also with the Ekklesia."[1]

In other words, the description of the Assembly life and practice given to us in the New Testament Acts of the Apostles and the Epistles are not just recorded for the sake of history but a pattern for believers. May the Lord help us to come to terms with this simple truth.

Let us again stress that God is very absolute when it comes to His divine pattern. He entertains no good ideas or suggestions for its improvement. Thrice in scripture, He warned, *"See that you follow strictly the pattern shown to you on the mount"* (Exodus 25:6, 40; Heb. 8:5). He has been seen to deal decisively with any form of breach of His blueprint. He killed the first two sons of Aaron in one swoop and demanded that their father make no lamentation. He spoilt David's fun as he was bringing the ark back to Jerusalem by killing Uzzar – it was over this same matter. No

---

[1] www.lordsrecovery.org/explanation

generation of Christianity is at liberty to introduce modifications to the divine pattern.

With all that has been said however, this is not primarily an attempt to discredit the existing structure of church as we know it but to point out beyond every reasonable doubt that the home assembly structure was the first structure utilised by followers of Christ (and probably nearest to the divine standard) and so should not be looked upon as strange. Often times, when people ask me what church I attend and I tell them I don't go to church but fellowship with brethren in homes, they throw up this puzzled look – especially in Nigeria. In our clime, the general mindset is that it is not possible for one to be a true Christian and not be the member of one church or the other.

The stark reality, however, is that in many parts of the world, including Nigeria, there is a staggering population of believers who are simply walking away from man-made organizations – not because they are backsliding but because, increasingly, they realise their commitment to the institutional church arrangement is an undue competition with their love and devotion to the Lord Jesus Christ and to God's eternal purpose. This book is actually targeting such believers; who are experiencing a growing discontent with the structure of church as we know it; whose hearts are yearning for the simplicity and purity of what they read about in the Acts of the Apostles; who are totally uneasy with the complexities of human organization and tradition that Christendom has been encumbered with; who feel drained of life with the myriads of religious activities week in, week out, all year long; and who long for an authentic organic fellowship with other believers under the Headship of the living and actively present Christ.

Such believers oftentimes feel, or are told, they have a problem; no, you don't have a problem. What you are feeling is actually a summon of the Spirit to experience Christ outside the walls of institutional religion. Press into Him the more; look out for like-minded saints to sharpen one another. Start to prioritise organic fellowship with the twos and the threes in the environment of everyday life. He is faithful; as many who seek will find. At the end of this book is a list of recommended reading that will help you in your quest.

CHAPTER FIVE

RECRUITING FAMILIES TO BE CENTRES OF KINGDOM ACTIVITY (HOME ASSEMBLIES) IN OUR LOCAL COMMUNITIES

Having gone this far in this book, we have come to the place of decision making, of making a commitment to become involved in God's vision of restoration. Yes, we all can be involved and it should start with a commitment to walking in truth and instructing your household in righteousness. As a parent, your God-assigned duty it is to show godly examples to your children by walking in unity with your spouse and bringing Heaven to earth in your family.

I cannot overemphasise the need for a regular family devotion in this vision. Sadly, however, in many homes, this has been reduced to a mere religious routine void of life. Your sincerity of heart as well as the sense of value you attach to your family altar and your commitment to same will determine the level of freshness and the degree of life that you will enjoy from it. Determine what time of the day works best for you; what matters the most is your consistency. Be creative; let each day be something new. Encourage fellowship and constant communication among family members.

Actually, it is in the family that the children are trained to cultivate an intimate personal walk with the risen, living and indwelling Christ, as they learn to pray, study the scriptures, hear the voice of God and walk by faith. In short, it is in the family that disciples are made and raised. It is a failure on the part of the parents if they abdicate this responsibility to their church. The whole essence of this book is to bring parents to realise that their home is the Ekklesia. And the sooner you realise and begin to see your home literally as the unit of the Assembly, the healthier for you and the better for God's divine purpose.

Stop seeing Ekklesia as where you go; see Ekklesia as your family and you, the parents, as the plural-overseer while every other person under your roof: biological children, house-helps, relatives etc. are the brethren with whom you fellowship. Just as pastors see it as their role to feed the flock with solid spiritual food, to pray constantly for them and ward off the activities of the stranger, the wolf and the thief, that exactly is our role as parents.

To deliberately cultivate the mind set of seeing your home as the Ekklesia, bring everything you do in church into your home. For instance, do you hold prayer meetings or bible study in church? Start holding such among members of your household right in your home. Do you go for evangelism in church? Take the initiative to do this as a family in your residential area. What makes you think communion can be served only in church? Break bread to remember the Lord right in your home with the members of your family.

Commitment Is Needed

Building a healthy home that truly functions as God's Ekklesia, requires commitment; this can't be overemphasized.

Unfortunately, organised church has been so structured to consume most of our time that there is hardly any time left to do anything else. Some people have to attend church as many as five times a week – some even more! What time do they have to function as the Ekklesia in their home? What time do they even have to service a personal relationship with the Lord? What time do they have to spend with their children in personally tutoring them in God's way? This is far from being healthy and such people will wake up 20 years down the road to discover that they have been spent in activity but with no corresponding depth in an authentic intimate fellowship with Christ.

Going forward, begin to proactively initiate conversations with your neighbours; those you can easily trek a few minutes to get to their place. This is what Henry Hon describes as "Greeting", a concept he developed from Romans 16.

Once you have constituted your own family/household to be an expression of the Assembly; and you are proactively greeting other believers in your neighbourhood, you should proceed to inviting these neighbours whom you have been relating with to come into your own home and share fellowship. Often times, some of these neighbours would have taken the initiative to reciprocate the visit even before you ask. You can open up your home once a month, twice a month or weekly – as the Lord gives you the grace. If you can, share some light refreshments in the meetings. Again, some of these neighbours will take the initiative to equally bring some refreshments to add to whatever you have provided. There is something mystical about eating together: it creates a warm, cordial and homely atmosphere and facilitates bonding.

In these home gatherings, focus strictly on the Lord. Don't stray into discussing politics or the economy or sports. Neither should it be a lecture where others sit down in passivity. Encourage participation; let the voice of the youngest child be heard. Let all contributions be warmly received. Encourage creativity in ministry as much as possible. Avoid bringing up contentious doctrines; let the fellowship and discussion centre on Christ and how He is being experienced by each and every one. I've observed that in participatory ministry, most of us end up teaching and hardly share our personal experiences of Christ and its transformative effect on different areas of our lives. Encourage this more than merely sharing bible knowledge.

Do not be tempted to use the gathering to invite the attendees to your church. Let it remain open to all believers in your immediate neighbourhood. Even unbelievers are welcome; as they see the corporate Christ in His Assembly, they fall down and testify that indeed God is among you.

As you develop consistency in doing this, bonding will overtime develop among the more regular saints. This bonding is the very heart of the Assembly life. They are beginning to develop a corporate spiritual identity as saints in that particular area. As you progress in that, it will soon evolve into nursing a corporate spiritual burden or vision for your neighbourhood. You are now beginning to seek simple and creative ways of expressing the testimony of Christ to the unsaved within your neighbourhood as well as bringing other believers into the practice of our oneness in Christ. Sincerely, a home assembly that has not come to this level of Kingdom responsibility might as well be a club house. The spirit of life within and among you will instruct you on when and how to do.

Organise informal outreaches from time to time within your immediate neighbourhood in a very creative way and not necessarily the traditional evangelistic mode. Methods which have been used include love feast, free medical treatment, free coaching school for students, film shows, neighbourhood service, even a novelty match. Whatever methods employed, be sure that it doesn't overshadow the main goal, which is lifting up Jesus so that He may draw men to Himself.

We won't get there overnight but we must all start from somewhere and keep at it. No one who sets his hand on this plough should think of looking back. We all need to consecrate ourselves to the Lord for this task. May our families become houses that change the world. May our families become an expression of God's Ekklesia in a world so desperately in need of its Saviour, amen.

HANDLING CONFLICTS IN A CHRISTIAN HOME

Mike Oye, *Ph.D*

Reproduced from "The Word Legacy: Best of Mike Oye's messages in print" edited by E. Amotsuka et al, Niu Nation Publishers 2009

The Christian home is the first expression of Christ's Assembly. I say this with all conviction: The Christian home is an Assembly. The Christian home is more important than your church denominations. God counts on your home more than He counts on your local church because the home is the nucleus for every spirituality, for character building, for training children in righteousness, for raising leaders, for increasing the Kingdom of God. Children have to be trained by parents; domestic staffs have to be influenced positively in that home by the parents. In-laws and relations have to be influenced positively by the parents who are the husband and wife in a home.

The husband is the senior pastor while the wife is his assistant pastor. Both are pastors in the home; they are shepherds. All who come into that home whether temporarily or permanently are sheep and lamb to be fed and tended by the two pastors. You have a unique position in your home.

For I have known [chosen] *him, in order that he may command his children and his household after him, that they keep the way of the Lord, to do righteousness and justice, that the Lord may bring to Abraham what He has spoken to him.* —Gen. 18:19

God chose Abraham so that he will give good leadership to his children and his household. Household involves everybody who comes into that home: housemaids, servants, in-laws, visitors and so on. And as a result of his good leadership, his children and household uphold the values of justice and judgment. Whereas these two words are closely related one to another, they mean different things. Justice is morality i.e. fair play. Jesus puts it this way: do unto others, as you would like others to do unto you.

Judgment is making right decisions, i.e. right thinking in the home, in public and so on. That is spirituality. Justice and judgment both summarize spirituality and godliness. He said, so that they may do these things in the public. Now, that means the home is the factory where we manufacture a brand new type of human beings to be injected into society. We prepare and incubate people through the words of God and through examples. We inject those people into society to take different positions and perform according to justice and judgment.

God says when Abraham does this, the blessings He had already promised him would come into fulfilment. So homes are blessed when the man who is in control acts like a real pastor representing God's mind in the family, with the support of the wife. I repeat - the home is the Assembly; the parent is a pastor and that parent is accountable unto God - this is fundamental. A pastor is supposed to set a godly example.

"And for their sakes I sanctify myself that also that they also might be sanctified through the truth." – John 17:19

Jesus the high priest, the greatest pastor, says, "For the sake of the children God has given me, I, their pastor, sanctify myself so that they, following my footsteps may also be sanctified." The pattern of God in teaching, discipling and bringing up other people to maturity is setting examples. The pastor is a pacesetter and a model, and he must focus on these two qualities all the time, otherwise he will allow self to come in and he may fail. The pastor is there not because of himself, but because of those who are following him. Jesus was conscious of this in His ministry. So, we are not there as physical parents alone, we are there as spiritual parents also. In fact, after we have given birth to the children physically, we need to lead them to be born again in the Spirit. We play a double role and each one of those roles is extremely important.

Having laid a foundation, let us to go to the basics. If there is no agreement between the leaders of the home, the husband and wife, nothing can go on well. There must be agreement. In Matthew 18:15, Jesus says *"If another believer sins against you, go privately and point out the faults."* One basic thing to note is the fact that believers commit sin. Most of us are like the modern Pharisees, you know? Many a times in the home, the attitude we have towards our partner is "I thought you were a believer; now I know you are not". This is one foundational reason conflicts remain unsolved. When one of the two partners thinks of the other as being impeccably and sinlessly perfect; so whatever he does which is not hundred percent right makes that person an unbeliever and the person stands condemned.

Once you think of your partner as imperfect because he or she did something wrong, the conflict remains and there is no forgiveness. But listen to Jesus speaking: *"If a fellow believer sins against you..."* The first principle to put down in conflict resolution is, nobody is sinlessly perfect. Have that at the back of your mind and readjust your attitude accordingly, if you want to maintain a smooth flowing atmosphere of love and peace in the home. Jesus said to Peter, "Before the cock crows twice, you will deny me three times, but don't worry, I have prayed for you".

That is the right attitude; give your partner that allowance that he or she can do wrong or make a mistake. When my wife does anything I consider wrong, I just swallow them because I love her sincerely. I don't love her because she is perfect, I love her because of who she is.

Get this second attitude right: love your spouse not because of what he or she does but because of who he or she is. These are two different paradigms. If your love or cooperation is based on what the other person does or does not do, the home will never be stable. Till you die, both of you will do things against each other - not deliberately, not to hurt yourselves but simply because you are you. That is the reason the Bible specifically says, *"Husbands, live with your wives with understanding"* (I Peter 3:7).

The conclusion of the matter here is that Christian men and women commit sins. Note, I did not say Christian men and women live in sin. The two statements are different. Look at verse 15 again: *"If another believer..."* That other believer is your partner.

In verse 21: *"Then Peter came to Jesus and asked, Lord, how often should I forgive someone who sins against me?"* This someone is your spouse. Peter was being very practical, because I believe he quickly looked at his home and remembered his wife and mother-in-law. Jesus replied: seventy times seven, four hundred and ninety times. What He meant is that one of the main remedies to conflicts is to always keep forgiving from the bottom of your heart.

Some people say they have forgiven but when another thing occurs the following day, they refer to history and they mention all the things of the past. In fact, I have seen some couples who will bring out diaries in which they wrote such offences and recall what happened on a particular date. What records are you keeping? That spirit of unforgiveness has terrible consequences.

Back to verse 15: *"If another believer sins against you, **go privately and point out the fault"**.*

Here is a big principle that leads to resolution of conflicts: **the one who is offended should be pro-active.** Don't wait to see whether your partner will realize what he/she did. So if one week passes, two weeks, one month and you are still waiting? Do you know what is happening? Your partner probably didn't even know but you are already nursing bitterness and anger. You will react to her in so many ways but he or she would not understand why you are reacting. The problems become complicated; not only are you bitter but you are keeping malice till you become sick. That sickness is psycho-somatic, if you go to the hospital, you won't be healed because it is not something that can be seen under the microscope. It is only diagnosed by the Spirit of God and you must co-operate with the Spirit for it to be diagnosed.

So for the poison to be expunged from your heart and your home, be pro-active. It is you who has been offended, yet the word of God says you should take the step to forgive the one who has offended you. Reveal the offence ion a spirit of meekness and reconciliation and your partner, under normal conditions, would say "I am sorry, I didn't know that I offended you, I am sorry." And he or she may explain everything that happened. And once that has been done, do what the bible says: *"Love believeth all things."* That is all.

The third principle is: **Never dwell on actions, dwell on motives.** There are times my wife does certain things and I just laugh. I have known one thing about her: her intentions are always right. So I don't take offence. She knows that if she had told me earlier I would disagree - my nature is not exactly her nature. God never puts two people together with the same nature in a home. You may have some things similar but let me tell you that if you go deep down, you will see two different people; the only thing that binds you is that two of you are children of God. When they say two shall be one it doesn't mean that the person has changed into you. You are two different people.

An action may look totally wrong to you; find out from your partner his or her intentions and by the time he or she explains and you know the motive you may find out there is no reason for conflict at all. If the other person listens, and confesses it, you have won that person back; you have gained your brother back. You know, whilst that conflict lasted, you were separated and that may leave room for all types of evil to come in.

If the other agrees and confesses, you have gained your brother or sister. Another important principle there again is humility. A couple came to me some time ago and we stayed awake till about 1am without making much progress because both couples wanted to be right throughout. Both of you cannot be hundred percent right. There must be something each party has contributed to the conflict. Allow the other partner to speak. The principle: *"Therefore my beloved brethren, let every man be swift to hear but slow to speak. Be slow to anger"* (James 1:19) must be upheld.

God made only one mouth but two ears. Why don't we listen twice before we speak once? Please listen to the 'foolishness'. And candidly, in most cases, it is the men who don't listen. The reason is that women are very slow and their speech is detailed but the men are not ready for details. But, you see, if details don't come out, the root of the problem will not be uncovered. Allow the women time to speak out their "foolishness". If you are too busy a man and you are result-oriented, please change that habit and find time in the night as long as you are at home to deliberately have one hour of lecture from your wife. By the time you practice this for about two weeks, it would become part of you.

This is how I learnt patience; I learnt it from my wife. Before our wedding, I thought I was one of the most patient and spiritual men in the world. But after our marriage and we started going to the market together, she would spend such a long time bargaining with the sellers (my wife cannot afford to waste one kobo while I can waste ten naira easily); this used to get me embarrassed.

However, she sat me down one day and gave me a thorough lecture. She said, "I am not doing this because I want to waste your time". At that time I was a Travelling Secretary for Scripture Union and my salary was rather small; yet we had to manage. My wife is a wonderful manager of resources and instead of me to appreciate that, I would be thinking of my own time. But after that wonderful lecture of showing me her motive for taking so much time in the market, I capitulated.

Subsequently, whenever I took her to the market, I began to go along with a good book and look for a comfortable place to stay and read. When I see her coming I will get up and open the boot for her, then she would apologise for keeping me waiting; but because I now understood her better, I would reply, 'Don't worry'. You see, understanding the other partner makes us mature spiritually. That is why in the private sector or civil service, when they want to take somebody for a key position that has to deal with personnel, they want somebody who has been married for a long time and possibly with children because they believe that he would have passed through that kind of training.

Let us learn patience from one another; let us be good listeners and let our words be few. Anger is not a good thing; impatience has done untold damage in many relationships. The crux here is that if it is you who offended the other person, you should be humble enough to accept your fault. Humility includes accepting faults. Many Christians are not ready to accept faults; this is nothing but pride. Pride goes before destruction; it is one of the sins God hates the most and will hinder our blessings and grace.

Once we are able to resolve conflicts, there will be agreement in the home and whenever you pray, the prayers will be answered. This is the secret. Concerning the couple I spoke of earlier, I found out that for thirteen years, they have never prayed together. Thirteen years of no agreement in prayer and never studying the word of God together! Where will the renewal of mind come from? One of the secrets of resolving conflicts is studying the word of God together as a couple.

In the family, there should be three ways of studying the word: personal study, couple's study and the family altar. The family altar is when all family members including visitors come together to study the word. After the family altar, the individuals can now study the word on their own for at least thirty minutes. When you come together like that to study and pray, you may only digest a verse of the scripture or you may analyze a whole passage together. As you do this, your minds become more and more integrated and many conflicts that could have occurred will not come up at all because you are one in mind.

When should we resolve conflicts? The answer from the word of God is on daily basis. *"Be angry but do not sin, do not let the sun go down upon you anger"*. Don't ever sleep at home with a conflict hanging. If you allow it to hang, you are planting a seed and when the seed takes root, it will be difficult to uproot.

If you are unable to resolve the conflict between you and your spouse, then we can go to verse 16:

> *"But if he will not hear, take with you one or two more, that 'by the mouth of two or three witnesses every word may be established.'"*

However, I pray you won't even get to this stage before the conflict is resolved amicably. Children of God miss a lot when the husband and wife don't trust and respect each other to resolve conflicts between them and the need to involve a third party or fourth party arises. My late wife and I got married in 1970; and till she was called home to glory in 2012, we never for once took any case to any man or any parent; nobody has ever come in to resolve any issue for us.

This does not mean that issues never arose but we both have the word of God and we study it. We have gone through the Bible so many times from Genesis to Revelation as individuals, as a couple and as a family. We know the mind of God and whenever there is conflict, we know what to say, where to go and how to pray about it. You are two pastors living together and therefore must learn how to resolve conflicts, if you cannot agree and resolve any conflicts with the person closest to you, how can you resolve conflicts outside the home?

1 Tim. 3:5 says, *"For if a man does not know how to rule his own house, how will he take care of the Assembly of God?"* This is one of the qualities of a pastor. If you cannot love the person who is closer to you, and love him/her with the love of God, forgiving and forgetting, how can you forgive other people outside the home? When two people are living together, one of them must become a fool. If I am the fool today, the example I have set will challenge the other person so that tomorrow the other person can also become a fool that the conflicts may be resolved.

Consider the life of Abraham with Lot. When there was a big conflict, rather than destroy the plan of God, Abraham, a very humble, loving and godly man called his nephew and told him, 'See, the land is before us; if you decide to take the right side I will take the left and if you decide to go left I will take the right'. Lot, on the other hand, was a self-centred man, so naturally, he took the right side which was full of rivers and lush grass for his cattle while the older man, who played the fool, took the left side. But God appeared to him and said, 'Because of your choice I am going to do something special'.

Make up your mind to gain back your spouse; let there be reconciliation in our lives and let those hurts, bitterness, and unforgiveness which are causing aches and pains in our lives be resolved. These aches and pains affect our children because they know and observe what goes on in the home.

But, in the event that the conflict in the home is very serious, there should be a third party. Seek for a man or a woman of high integrity in God because when you begin to expose your weaknesses onto another person, if the person is not pure or loving in spirit, he or she may ruin things rather than mend them. In fact, you will find some people who will take advantage of your situation and cause more harm in the family.

Let us look at verse 18: *"Verily I say unto you, whatsoever you shall bind on earth shall be bound in heaven, and whatsoever you shall loose on earth shall be loosed in heaven"*. When both husband and wife have resolved the conflicts, their prayers become highly effective to draw the blessings, miracles and so on. It is further buttressed in Matthew 18:19: *"Again I say unto you, that if two of you* (husband and wife) *shall agree on earth as touching anything that they shall ask, it shall be done for them of my Father which is in heaven"*.

You can see that Jesus is repeating Himself. He is laying an emphasis. When Jesus says verily, verily, it means a lot; it is a fundamental fact in the Kingdom. This is the basis for the progress in the home. God is seated on the throne and looking at the two of you. When you follow this biblical principle for conflict resolution, and the causative agent for schism and separation has been dealt with, unity is restored in the home and God commands His blessings where there is unity (Psalm 133).

Therefore, for real shalom and total holistic well-being to reign in the home, there must be agreement between husband and wife. Later on in vs. 20, Jesus says *"For where two or three are gathered together in My name, I am there in the midst of them."* He is now extending that to your children. When you ask for things in the family altar, miracles will naturally result and when the children begin to see that some of the prayers raised at the family altar are being answered, their faith in God will increase.

I have children who are living with me whose faith challenges me; young people of 21 to 23 years, doing exploits; but they learnt all these from our living room. They have been to the polytechnic and universities and yet they practice all those things they have learnt from home there. Let our unity and agreement raise up children that would go into the community to change the situation in Nigeria. The home is extremely important and you are a special pastor in your home.

Reproduced with permission.

It's been 20 years since the Lord first brought the article below across our way, while on campus in Ogbomoso, Oyo state, Nigeria. The Lord granted us understanding into its simple message and also gave us the privilege of experiencing the community life of the Ekklesia that it describes. With so much excitement about this treasure which we found, we reproduced and distributed this article in the thousands for others to also gain the same insight and hopefully be led into the same experience of community life.

Over the years, as we interacted with various groups and initiatives within the Body of Christ and as we met many dear believers genuinely concerned about the state of the Body, we get more convinced that the greatest challenge for Christendom today is letting go of the old wineskin/structure and intentionally returning to the model so detailedly shown in the New Testament writs. As Paul Rapoza puts it, *"God started the church (Assembly) the way He wanted it; now He wants the church (Assembly) the way He started it"*. It's our prayer that as you read through these 15 theses, your heart will encounter truth afresh and you will be one of those whom the Lord will use to re-establish His true pattern for Assembly life.

"15 Theses" For A New Reformation
By Wolfgang Simson

God is changing the Assembly, and that, in turn, will change the world. Millions of Christians around the world are aware of an imminent reformation of global proportions. They say, in effect: "Ekklesia as we know it is preventing Ekklesia as God wants it." A growing number of them are surprisingly hearing God say the very same things. There is a collective new awareness of age-old revelations, a corporate spiritual echo. In the following "15 Theses" I will summarize a part of this, and I am convinced that it reflects a part of what the Spirit of God is saying to the Ekklesia today. For some, it might be the proverbial fist-sized cloud on Elijah's sky. Others already feel the pouring rain.

1. Church is a Way of Life, not a series of religious meetings

Before they were called Christians, followers of Christ have been called "The Way". One of the reasons was that they have literally found "the way to live." The nature of Ekklesia is not reflected in a constant series of religious meetings lead by professional clergy in holy rooms specially reserved to experience Jesus, but in the prophetic way followers of Christ live their everyday life in spiritually extended families as a vivid answer to the questions society faces, at the place where it counts most: in their homes.

2. Time to change the system

In aligning itself to the religious patterns of the day, the historic Orthodox Church after Constantine in the 4th century AD adopted a religious system which was in essence Old Testament, complete with priests, altar, a Christian temple (cathedral), frankincense and a Jewish, synagogue-style worship pattern. The Roman Catholic Church went on to canonize the system. Luther did reform the content of the gospel, but left the outer forms of "church" remarkably untouched; the Free-Churches freed the system from the State, the Baptists then baptized it, the Quakers dry-cleaned it, the Salvation Army put it into a uniform, the Pentecostals anointed it and the Charismatic renewed it, but until today nobody has really changed the superstructure. It is about time to do just that.

3. The Third Reformation.

In rediscovering the gospel of salvation by faith and grace alone, Luther started to reform Christendom through a reformation of theology. In the 18th century through movements like the Moravians there was a recovery of a new intimacy with God, which led to a reformation of spirituality, the Second Reformation. Now God is touching the wineskins themselves, initiating a Third Reformation, a reformation of structure.

4. From *Church*-Houses to house-*churches*

Since New Testament times, there is no such thing as "a house of God". At the cost of his life, Stephen reminded unequivocally: God does not live in temples made by human hands. The Church is the people of God. The Ekklesia, therefore, was and is at home where people are at home: in ordinary houses. There, the people of God:

- Share their lives in the power of the Holy Spirit,
- Have "meatings," that is, they eat when they meet,
- They often do not even hesitate to sell private property and share material and spiritual blessings,
- Teach each other in real-life situations how to obey God's word, dialogue - and not professor-style,
- Pray and prophesy with each other, baptize, `lose their face' and their ego by confessing their sins,
- Regaining a new corporate identity by experiencing love, acceptance and forgiveness.

5. The Assembly gatherings have to become small in order to grow big

Most churches of today are simply too big to provide real fellowship. They have too often become "fellowships without fellowship." The New Testament Assembly was a mass of small groups, typically between 10 and 15 people. It grew not upward into big congregations between 20 and 300 people filling a cathedral and making real, mutual communication improbable. Instead, it multiplied "sideward", like organic cells, once these groups reached around 15-20 people. Then, if possible, it drew all the Christians together into citywide celebrations, as with Solomon's Temple court in Jerusalem. The traditional congregational church as we know it is, statistically speaking, neither big nor beautiful, but rather a sad compromise, an overgrown house-church and an under-grown celebration, often missing the dynamics of both.

6. No Assembly is led by a Pastor alone

The local assembly is not led by a Pastor, but fathered by an Elder, a local person of wisdom and reality. The local home-assemblies are then networked into a movement by the combination of elders and members of the so-called five-fold ministries (Apostles, Prophets, Pastors, Evangelists and Teachers) circulating "from house to house," whereby there is a special foundational role to play for the apostolic and prophetic ministries (Eph. 2:20, and 4:11.12). A Pastor (shepherd) is a very necessary part of the whole team, but he cannot fulfill more than a part of the whole task of "equipping the saints for the ministry," and has to be complemented synergistically by the other four ministries in order to function properly.

7. The right pieces - fitted together in the wrong way

In doing a puzzle, we need to have the right original for the pieces, otherwise the final product, the whole picture, turns out wrong, and the individual pieces do not make much sense. This has happened to large parts of the Christian world: we have all the right pieces, but have fitted them together wrong, because of fear, tradition, religious jealousy and a power-and-control mentality. As water is found in three forms, ice, water and steam, the five ministries mentioned in Eph. 4:11-12, the Apostles, Prophets, Pastors, Teachers and Evangelists are also found today, but not always in the right forms and in the right places: they are often frozen to ice in the rigid system of institutionalized Christianity; they sometimes exist as clear water; or they have vanished like steam into the thin air of free-flying ministries and "independent" churches, accountable to no-one. As it is best to water flowers with the fluid version of water, these five equipping ministries will have to be transformed back into new, and at the same time age-old, forms, so that the whole spiritual organism can flourish and the individual "ministers" can find their proper role and place in the whole. That is one more reason why we need to return to the Maker's original and blueprint for the Ekklesia.

8. God does not leave the Assembly in the hands of bureaucratic clergy

No expression of a New Testament assembly is ever led by just one professional "holy man" doing the business of communicating with God and then feeding some relatively passive religious consumers Moses-style. Christianity has adopted this method from pagan religions, or at best from the Old Testament. The heavy professionalisation of Christendom since Constantine has now been a pervasive influence long enough, dividing the people of God artificially into laity and clergy. According to the New Testament (1 Tim. 2:5), *"there is one God, and one mediator also between God and men, the man Christ Jesus."* God simply does not bless religious professionals to force themselves in-between people and God forever. The veil is torn, and God is allowing people to access Himself directly through Jesus Christ, the only Way. To enable the priesthood of all believers, the present system will have to change completely. Bureaucracy is the most dubious of all administrative systems, because it basically asks only two questions: yes or no. There is no room for spontaneity and humanity, no room for real life. This may be OK for politics and companies, but not the Lord's Ekklesia. God seems to be in the business of delivering His Ekklesia from a Babylonian captivity of religious bureaucrats and controlling spirits into the public domain, the hands of ordinary people made extraordinary by God, who, like in the old days, may still smell of fish, perfume and revolution.

9. Return from organized to organic forms of Christianity

The "Body of Christ" is a vivid description of an organic, not an organized, being. Ekklesia consists on its local level of a multitude of spiritual families, which are organically related to each other as a network, where the way the pieces are functioning together is an integral part of the message of the whole. What has become a maximum of organization with a minimum of organism, has to be changed into a minimum of organization to allow a maximum of organism. Too much organization has, like a straightjacket, often choked the organism for fear that something might go wrong. Fear is the opposite of faith, and not exactly a Christian virtue. Fear wants to control, faith can trust. Control, therefore, may be good, but trust is better. The Body of Christ is entrusted by God into the hands of steward-minded people with a supernatural charismatic gift to believe God that He is still in control, even if they are not. A development of trust-related regional and national networks, not a new arrangement of political ecumenism is necessary for organic forms of Christianity to re-emerge.

10. From worshipping our worship to worshipping God

The image of much of contemporary Christianity can be summarized, a bit euphemistically, as holy people coming regularly to a holy place at a holy day at a holy hour to participate in a holy ritual lead by a holy man dressed in holy clothes against a holy fee. Since this regular performance-oriented enterprise called "worship service" requires a lot of organizational talent and administrative bureaucracy to keep going, formalized and institutionalized patterns developed quickly into rigid traditions. Statistically, a traditional 1-2 hour "worship service" is very resource-hungry but actually produces very little fruit in terms of discipling people, that is, in changed lives. Economically speaking, it might be a "high input and low output" structure. Traditionally, the desire to "worship in the right way" has led to much denominationalism, confessionalism and nominalism. This not only ignores that Christians are called to "worship in truth and in spirit," not in cathedrals holding songbooks, but also ignores that most of life is informal, and so is Christianity as "the Way of Life." Do we need to change from being powerful actors to start "acting powerfully?"

11. Stop bringing people to *church* (the building); start bringing the *church* (Ekklesia) to the people

The Ekklesia is changing back from being a Come-structure to being again a Go-structure. As one result, the Ekklesia needs to stop trying to bring people "into the *church*," and start bringing the Ekklesia to the people. The mission of the Ekklesia will never be accomplished just by adding to the existing structure; it will take nothing less than a mushrooming of the Ekklesia through spontaneous multiplication of itself into areas of the population of the world, where Christ is not yet known.

12. Rediscovering the "Lord's Supper" to be a real supper with real food

Church tradition has managed to "celebrate the Lord's Supper" in a homeopathic and deeply religious form, characteristically with a few drops of wine, a tasteless cookie and a sad face. However, the "Lord's Supper" was actually more a substantial supper with a symbolic meaning, than a symbolic supper with a substantial meaning. God is restoring eating back into our meeting.

13. From Denominations to city-wide celebrations

Jesus called a universal movement, and what came was a series of religious companies with global chains marketing their special brands of Christianity and competing with each other. Through this branding of Christianity, most of Protestantism have, therefore, become politically insignificant and often more concerned with traditional specialties and religious infighting than with developing a collective testimony before the world. Jesus simply never asked people to organize themselves into denominations. In the early days of the Ekklesia, Christians had a dual identity: they were truly His Assembly and vertically converted to God, and then organized themselves according to geography, that is, converting also horizontally to each other on earth. This means not only Christian neighbours organizing themselves into neighbourhood - or home-assemblies, where they share their lives locally, but Christians coming together as a collective identity as much as they can for citywide or regional celebrations expressing the corporateness of the Ekklesia of the city or region. Authenticity in the neighbourhoods connected with a regional or citywide corporate identity will make the Church not only politically significant and spiritually convincing, but will allow a return to the biblical model of the City-Ekklesia.

14. Developing a persecution-proof spirit

They crucified Jesus, the Boss of all the Christians. Today, His followers are often more into titles, medals and social respectability, or, worst of all, they remain silent and are not worth being noticed at all. *"Blessed are you when you are persecuted"*, says Jesus. Biblical Christianity is a healthy threat to pagan godlessness and sinfulness, a world overcome by greed, materialism, jealousy and any amount of demonic standards of ethics, sex, money and power. Contemporary Christianity in many countries is simply too harmless and polite to be worth persecuting.

But as Christians again live out New Testament standards of life and, for example, call sin as sin, conversion or persecution has been, is and will be the natural reaction of the world. Instead of nesting comfortably in temporary zones of religious liberty, Christians will have to prepare to be again discovered as the main culprits against global humanism, the modern slavery of having to have fun and the outright worship of Self, the wrong centre of the universe. That is why Christians will and must feel the "repressive tolerance" of a world which has lost any absolutes and therefore refuses to recognize and obey its creator God with His absolute standards. Coupled with the growing ideologisation, privatization and spiritualisation of politics and economics, Christians will, sooner than most think, have their chance to stand happily accused in the company of Jesus. They need to prepare now for the future by developing a persecution-proof spirit and an even more persecution-proof structure.

15. The Ekklesia comes home

Where is the easiest place, say, for a man to be spiritual? Maybe again, is it hiding behind a big pulpit, dressed up in holy robes, preaching holy words to a faceless crowd and then disappearing into an office? And what is the most difficult, and therefore most meaningful, place for a man to be spiritual? At home, in the presence of his wife and children, where everything he does and says is automatically put through a spiritual litmus test against reality, where hypocrisy can be effectively weeded out and authenticity can grow. Much of Christianity has fled the family, often as a place of its own spiritual defeat, and then has organized artificial performances in sacred buildings far from the atmosphere of real life. As God is in the business of recapturing the homes, the Assembly turns back to its roots, back to where it came from. It literally comes home, completing the circle of *Church* history at the end of world history.

As Christians of all walks of life, from all denominations and backgrounds, feel a clear echo in their spirit to what God's Spirit is saying to the Assembly, and start to hear globally in order to act locally, they begin to function again as one body. They organize themselves into neighbourhood home-assemblies and meet in regional or city-celebrations. You are invited to become part of this movement and make your own contribution. Maybe your home, too, will become a house that changes the world.

This article as well as Wolfgang Simson's book, Houses that changed the world, can be downloaded free from the Internet.

IS "CHURCH" REALLY THE SAME AS "EKKLESIA"?

An ancient Chinese proverb says the beginning of wisdom is to call things by their proper names. A name represents identity. An identity crisis is inevitable when names are tampered with; and this is what the Body of Christ has suffered for so long in history. However, in this season of light, the Lord is bringing startling revelations to limelight which should concern every sincere Christian. It has to do with the word, "Church"; the excerpt below explains more. After reading, you should please ask yourself if you will like to continue with the error simply because it has become entrenched; or you will choose to align with truth. God bless you as you read:

Defining Church and Assembly

An Excerpt from ONE: Unfolding God's Eternal Purpose from House to House, by Henry Hon, 2016, pg 10-11

Since the matter of "church" is probably the biggest item of Christianity after faith in Jesus Christ, it is impossible to be reset back to the beginning without receiving fresh eyes on this matter of church. To begin with, the word "church" in the Bible is a mistranslation from the Greek word *ekklesia*. The accurate translation is "assembly" or "congregation." Literally, *ekklesia* means the "called out ones." The common usage of this word during the apostles' time was for a called out assembly of people, such as a town square meeting, whose citizens were "called out" to attend. Therefore, the correct translation of *ekklesia* is assembly, or congregation (Thayer's Greek Lexicon).

The word "church" actually comes from a very different Greek word. The etymology (etymology.com) of the word "church" is said to be from *kyriake (oikia)*, or *kyriakon doma* meaning, "the lord's house." It refers to an actual place of worship, which included a place to worship idols. This word started being used to identify a Christian place of worship around the fourth century AD, when Constantine established Christianity as the Roman state religion. It was during this time that Christians began meeting in dedicated worship buildings, rather than in homes or in public places.

In 1525, William Tyndale translated the first printed Bible into English. He translated the word *ekklesia* as "congregation" or assembly. This was in direct contradiction to the Roman Church. At that time, the Roman Church feared that removing the word "church" from the Bible would threaten their authority and hierarchy. This was one of the major reasons Tyndale was killed and burned at the stake by the Roman Church in 1536. When King James authorized his translation of the Bible in 1611, eighty-four percent of the New Testament was translated directly from Tyndale's Bible. But King James made one translation rule clear: *ekklesia* was to be translated "church" and not "congregation" or "assembly."

King James was the head of the Church of England (the Anglican church) and all forty-seven translators were members. Once again, for political and control reasons, the King James Version of the Bible mistranslated the Greek word *ekklesia* to "church." Since then, just about every English version of the Bible has kept to this translation of "church."

It is much simpler and honest when words are used exactly for what they mean. Even today the primary dictionary meaning of church is "a building that is used for Christian religious services" (Merriam-Webster). Christians who are more advanced in seeing the body of Christ (Eph. 1:22–23) have to constantly clarify and redefine "church" as the believers, not the building.

Considering this, for the sake of accuracy and in support of Tyndale who gave his life for the translation of the Bible, for this book, the word for ekklesia will be translated "assembly." When the word "church" is used, it will refer to either a physical place for Christian worship or an organized group of Christians associated with one or more dedicated physical buildings for worship.

AUTHOR'S NOTE

BE ENCOURAGED TO CONTACT ME if you've been blessed in any way by this book; I am eager to read your comments and testimonies. Similarly, if you seek clarification on any of the issues raised; or you want further guidance in making your home a centre of Kingdom activity or you are in a position to facilitate a seminar in your neighborhood, fellowship or institution; or if you are interested in teaming up with others who are running with this vision - my lines are open to you.

The good Lord bless you as you seek to be relevant to His Kingdom agenda.

In Kingdom pursuit,

ADEYEMO Temidayo
temidayo.adeyemo@gmail.com
+2348038548073, +2349067091964
Facebook page: Project Ekklesia, Nigeria
Website: Essencerestored.org

OTHER HELPFUL READINGS:

1. Houses that changed the world *by Wolfgang Simson*

2. Revolution: Story of the Early Church *by Gene Edwards*

3. One Ekklesia: The Practice of God's Eternal Purpose *by Henry Hon*

4. God's Favorite Place on Earth *by Frank Viola*

5. The Community Life of God *by Milt Rodriguez*

9 789785 001235